Understanding
The Great Gatsby

The Greenwood Press "Literature in Context" Series

UNDERSTANDING

The Great Gatsby

A STUDENT CASEBOOK TO ISSUES, SOURCES, AND HISTORICAL DOCUMENTS

Dalton Gross
and
MaryJean Gross

The Greenwood Press
"Literature in Context" Series
Claudia Durst Johnson, Series Editor

GREENWOOD PRESS
Westport, Connecticut • London

Library of Congress Cataloging-in-Publication Data

Gross, Dalton, 1936–
    Understanding The great Gatsby : a student casebook to issues,
sources, and historical documents / Dalton Gross and MaryJean Gross.
        p.   cm. — (The Greenwood Press "Literature in context"
series, ISSN 1074–598X)
    Includes bibliographical references and index.
    ISBN 0–313–30097–6 (alk. paper)
    1. Fitzgerald, F. Scott (Francis Scott), 1896–1940.   Great Gatsby—
Sources.   2. Literature and history—United States—History—20th
century—Sources.   I. Gross, MaryJean.   II. Title.   III. Series.
PS3511.I9G846   1998
813'.52—dc21   98–12146

British Library Cataloguing in Publication Data is available.

Library of Congress Catalog Card Number: 98–12146
ISBN: 0–313–30097–6
ISSN: 1074–598X

First published in 1998

Greenwood Press, 88 Post Road West, Westport, CT 06881
An imprint of Greenwood Publishing Group, Inc.

Printed in the United States of America

∞

The paper used in this book complies with the
Permanent Paper Standard issued by the National
Information Standards Organization (Z39.48-1984).

10 9 8 7 6 5 4 3 2

Contents

Introduction

Very few books have haunted the American imagination like F. Scott Fitzgerald's *The Great Gatsby*. Though it was published in 1925, both high school and college students can still relate to it, and it is very popular with teachers and professors. New biographies and critical works about Fitzgerald and his wife Zelda are published year after year. Between 1990 and 1996 alone, for example, 165 scholarly items came out about Fitzgerald and his work. Three film versions of *The Great Gatsby* have appeared: an unsuccessful silent film, a 1949 production starring Alan Ladd and Betty Field, and a 1974 version starring Robert Redford and Mia Farrow. This last film is remarkable for its visual interpretation of the 1920s. Seeing the lavish houses, the exotic clothes, and the expensive cars in the movie makes it easy for one to imagine how Gatsby, Daisy, and the others might look. A slowly moving film, it is nonetheless an elegant feast for the eyes.

Yet *The Great Gatsby* did not begin as a success. It sold only 25,000 copies in 1925, and very few for a long time after that. Some literary critics praised it, but the majority of newspaper reviewers were not impressed, and it went out of print in the 1930s. When Fitzgerald died in 1940, all of his books were out of print, and he was working as a Hollywood script writer. Debt-ridden, in bad health, and an alcoholic, he sometimes drunkenly accused strangers of thinking he was dead; it seemed likely at the time that this magnificent novel would disappear from the American scene and that its author would be completely forgotten.

But editions of *The Great Gatsby* began to appear again during the 1940s, and in the 1950s a full-scale Fitzgerald revival began (a revival concentrating on *The Great Gatsby*), which now continues more enthusiastically than ever. By 1980, 8 million copies of Fitzgerald's books had been sold, and 300,000 copies of *The Great Gatsby* were selling every year. What accounts for the powerful and lasting appeal of this novel? No single book can give a complete answer to that question. We can touch on some of the reasons here, though. For one thing, we can examine Fitzgerald's brilliant craftsmanship. And we can explore the author's personal background and the backdrop of the novel, the period of American history often called the "Roaring Twenties."

At its simplest the novel is about something familiar to most readers: a disillusioning, excruciatingly painful experience with love. But it is much more than that. The love story is intertwined with the force of the American Dream, as Fitzgerald understood it and as he saw it in the colorful and violent world of the 1920s; it is also intertwined with the personal crises of the author, which are now so well known that they are almost a part of popular culture. Yet none of these things would have had much impact on the popularity of the novel if it had not been for the author's guiding talent; F. Scott Fitzgerald is one of the greatest literary craftsmen that America has ever produced.

This book examines *The Great Gatsby* as a literary work. What techniques are employed? What makes the novel work? What is the overall effect on the reader? Because Fitzgerald's writing is heavily autobiographical, we will also look into the relationship between the novel and his life experiences. F. Scott and Zelda Fitzgerald led such intriguing lives that people are sometimes inclined to pay as much attention to their personal experiences as to their writing. We will look at their lives in this book, but only in terms of their influence on Fitzgerald's fiction.

For such an easy-to-read novel, *The Great Gatsby* is very rich and complex. Our understanding of it can be deepened and enriched by looking at the historical period in which it is set. Much that was familiar to the reader of the 1920s is no longer common knowledge. Newspaper and magazine articles as well as testimony from criminal trials and Senate hearings of the era will be used to re-create crucial aspects of the world Fitzgerald was depicting.

Because Jay Gatsby is, after all, a criminal, we will examine some of the major underworld figures and real criminal activities Fitzgerald drew on for his story, including the sort of New York night life created by Prohibition. Fitzgerald made skillful use of the scandals of the era—some briefly mentioned or just hinted at—to create the mood and tone he was seeking. Included in this book are documents on one of the worst scandals in the history of American sports, the fixing of the 1919 World Series, and on the greatest political scandal of Warren Gamaliel Harding's administration, the Teapot Dome case.

The lives of F. Scott and Zelda Fitzgerald, like the scandals of the 1920s, show how greatly values had changed since before World War I. Especially notable were changes in the social and economic roles women played and were expected to play. We will take a look at the "flapper," the newly emancipated American girl whom Fitzgerald wrote about so often that people mistakenly thought he had invented the term. *The Great Gatsby* is, in part, about marriage problems, and for that reason new attitudes toward marriage and sex will also be examined.

Fitzgerald did not think of himself as the sort of writer who set out to teach a lesson. He was concerned with telling a complicated story in a very striking way. Still, the fact remains that *The Great Gatsby* has a message. It has an impact on the thinking and value systems of its readers and makes them ask questions: What is Fitzgerald saying about the values of his society? What is he saying about the human condition? How does any of this relate to us today?

To a large extent, the answers to these questions can be found by examining *The Great Gatsby* in its literary and historical context. Quotations from *The Great Gatsby* are taken from Matthew J. Bruccoli, ed., *The Great Gatsby: The Authorized Text* (New York: Simon and Schuster, 1995).

1

Literary Analysis: What Makes *The Great Gatsby* Great

The Great Gatsby is a very popular novel, and today nearly all critics agree that it is a great one. But what makes it great? What elements set it apart? Many novels are so poorly written that they are never even published, and most that are published do not sell especially well. Of those that have good sales, good reviews, or both, most are soon forgotten. But a few become a permanent part of our literature. Why has *The Great Gatsby* become one of those few?

Probably no one is able to give a complete answer to that question. The things that make a book great are subtle and complicated. Perhaps some of them are indefinable. But we can at least touch on some of the basic elements that make *The Great Gatsby* what it is and on some of the meanings it has for perceptive readers.

One can read *The Great Gatsby* easily and enjoyably without careful analysis. The essential story seems simple enough. Yet readers who stop to ask themselves exactly why they enjoyed the novel, what makes it work, will find themselves looking at a very complex book that means much more than it seems to at first glance. The novel has nearly perfect unity of effect. Every image, every character, every symbol, every turn of the plot contributes to the theme and to the feeling one carries away from reading it, even though one may not always be consciously aware of their influence. Let us begin with an overly simplified statement of the theme: the dangerously misguided nature of Gatsby's worship of the monied world of Daisy Buchanan. As we come to see how Fitzgerald develops this theme, we will also come to see how much depth and richness it actually has.

Taken by itself, the plot is simple and bears out what has just been said about the theme of the novel in a flat, anecdotal way. Gatsby, a poor young man, falls in love with a rich girl while he is serving as an officer in the army during World War I. She loves him but marries someone else when she has given up on his coming back to her. She does not realize that he is poor. He becomes rich through bootlegging and other crimes, finds her, and tries to persuade her to leave her husband for him. She nearly does, but instead stays with her husband. She kills her husband's mistress in an automobile accident, and the dead woman's husband, deceived into thinking Gatsby is responsible, kills Gatsby and then himself. The reader is left uncertain as to what extent Gatsby's former love is involved in the deception. Gatsby has been rejected by the woman he loves and, quite possibly, betrayed by her.

But to know this is to have only the slightest inkling of what *The Great Gatsby* is all about. A good beginning point for understanding the novel is to look at how the plot unfolds through one of the chief unifying elements, the narrative point of view. Two things about the narrative structure are important here. First, everything the reader learns comes through Nick Carraway—either through Nick's own experience or what he has learned from others. Nick narrates the events of the story not in the order they occur, but in the order Fitzgerald wants them presented. Second, and at least as important, the events are described as Nick sees them. All the complex attitudes and emotions that contribute to the tone of the novel are conveyed to the reader through Nick's consciousness.

This brings us to the basic question about any first-person narrative: To what extent does the author wish us to accept the narrator's point of view? Often a writer achieves very strong effects through the contrast between what the narrator says and what the author makes the reader see. Huckleberry Finn is a classic example of this sort of narrator. Did any reader ever appreciate Emmeline Grangerford's poetry the way Huck does? Even if the narrator is intelligent, honest, and perceptive, what he sees will be colored by his own experiences and his own personality.

Does Fitzgerald, then, wish us to accept Nick's judgments? The answer to that is a qualified yes. Nick's opinions about Gatsby and the other major characters are meant to be accurate. But at the same time, as we will see later, Nick's world view does not serve him well. He calls himself honest, and, unlike many people who say that about themselves, he seems to be so. He thinks of himself as able to reserve judgment about others. He is aloof and cynical but fundamentally good-hearted. He is very intelligent and very smooth socially, with the self-confidence that comes from an established social position. All of these qualities contribute to his very highly developed moral sense.

But for all his honesty, Nick himself has been nearly destroyed by the events he relates, and his state of mind colors everything he says. He has been left lonely and directionless, with no faith in anything. To use a word that did not become popular until long after *The Great Gatsby* was written, he is alienated. Before he meets Gatsby he is already detached and at loose ends. He turns thirty in the course of the novel. He is unmarried and has no profession or specific ambition. He has come to the East with a rather lukewarm intention of going into the bond business, and has left behind a girl for whom he has no stronger feeling than friendliness to whom he wishes to avoid commitment. Like Gatsby, he has gone through World War I, a permanently disorienting experience for many men of his generation. In 1922, four years after the war, he still feels unsettled.

But his earlier basic disorientation is mild compared to the state in which he tells Gatsby's story. He has given up on the bond business and returned to the West, where he wants "no more riotous excursions with privileged glimpses into the human heart" (6). His experiences with Gatsby "temporarily closed out my interest in the abortive sorrows and short-winded elations of men" (7). In the hotel room where Tom Buchanan confronts Gatsby, Nick remembers chillingly that it is his birthday and that he is thirty, and contemplates the coming years of aging bachelorhood. He thinks for the moment that he wants Jordan Baker, but rejects her when she reacts with self-absorbed callousness to Myrtle Wilson's death. This insight into Jordan's essential selfishness completes his emotional isolation from everyone but Gatsby.

It is in this state of mind that Nick tells Gatsby's story. He rivets the reader's attention by saying that he left the East disillusioned with everything but Gatsby, yet he says Gatsby "represented everything for which I have an unaffected scorn" (6). At the same time, he finds Gatsby's "heightened sensitivity to the promises of life" "gorgeous" (6). Gradually the reader is led through the stages of Nick's growing knowledge of Gatsby. Gatsby is at first a fabulously rich neighbor who throws lavish, wild, glittering, chaotic parties in his mansion. The rumors about him are also wild, glittering, and chaotic: that he was a German spy and that he is a murderer.

When he meets Gatsby, Nick hears from him a preposterous version of his past life; this skewed biographical sketch is the origin of the ambivalence Nick feels. He almost laughs at Gatsby's story, but when Gatsby shows him his war medals and a picture of himself at Oxford, Nick decides the story must be true. From this point on he wishes to believe in Gatsby, in spite of all the evidence to the contrary. Later, when Tom Buchanan questions that Gatsby went to Oxford and Gatsby explains that as a United States Army officer he went there for a few months after the war, Nick wants to slap him on the back for justifying himself. However, the reader remembers what Nick has, ironically, forgotten—that Gatsby told him his family had gone to Oxford for generations. Gatsby is a man who says his family comes from San Francisco and says San Francisco is in the Midwest.

After hearing Gatsby's autobiography and forming a favorable opinion of him, Nick is jolted to learn that Gatsby is an associate of Meyer Wolfsheim, a man with firsthand knowledge of the death of Rosy Rosenthal, one of the most notorious of New York's gangland murders. Nick is told that Wolfsheim fixed the World Series and is "staggered" to learn that "one man could . . . play with the faith of fifty million people" (78). Here, as in fact all through the novel, American imagination and idealism have been betrayed.

Almost immediately Nick is exposed to another aspect of Gatsby, as he learns from Jordan Baker of his passionate love for Daisy Buchanan, and then sees Gatsby, in what is perhaps the most touching scene in the book, meeting Daisy again for the first time in five years, more tense, frightened, and awkward than a young boy on his first date. After relating this powerful scene, Nick tells the reader what he learned only much later—the story of Gatsby's early poverty and his experiences with Dan Cody. It is the juxtaposition of this earlier Gatsby with the later, with the sensitivities they have in common blurred and soiled by the development of a criminal personality, that gives *The Great Gatsby* some of its haunting, once-read-never-forgotten quality.

Finally, in a hotel room with Tom and Daisy Buchanan, Jordan Baker, and Gatsby, Nick must face the truth. Gatsby is a large-scale criminal. He is, among other things, a bootlegger. Moreover, he sees nothing wrong with what he does. Everything readers have guessed about Gatsby is now clear. He has lied to Nick from the very beginning. Gatsby, it seems, is everything Nick disapproves of. Nick is honest and cultivated and a practitioner of the social decencies. Gatsby is a liar and a criminal. He is ignorant and without taste. He is too raw to understand that the money he acquired as a criminal does not bridge the gap between his world and that of the Buchanans. Yet for Nick his friendship with Gatsby is the only redeeming experience of his time in the East. Why?

To answer that question is to go to the very heart of *The Great Gatsby*. Nick loves Gatsby's yearning, his imaginative idealism, his reaching for some indefinable glamorous goal. Early in the novel Nick calls it "an extraordinary gift for hope, a romantic readiness" (6). Yet Nick despises all that Gatsby stands for. Gatsby's idealism is entirely misdirected. He worships a sort of life that he thinks comes with great wealth. To him it is a life filled with wonder, excitement, fine things, and absolute self-worth. Gatsby's vision is a crude, corrupted form of the American Dream. If one has a vast amount of money, one becomes a wonderful person and enjoys a wonderful existence. For Gatsby, Daisy Buchanan is the embodiment of that life. His failure becomes tragic as he is destroyed by what he has pursued and loved so innocently and wholeheartedly.

For Nick, and for Fitzgerald, the American Dream in his time has become a dead and hollow thing. If the goal is simply wealth, then those who have wealth should be splendid, happy people. But Nick's final judgment of the Buchanans and of Jordan Baker is devastating. He tells Gatsby, "They're a rotten crowd. . . . You're worth the whole damn bunch put together" (162).

From the beginning Nick feels reservations about these people; eventually he comes to feel a deep aversion to them. Tom Buchanan is almost a caricature of the American Dream. He is wealthy and physically powerful. He has played football excellently at an Ivy League school, and he has married a beautiful woman. But he is also stupid, brutal, and bored, mouthing ideas he has stolen and cannot even remember correctly from third-rate books. Nick learns of his infidelity and watches him break his mistress' nose for mentioning Daisy's name. Nick guesses correctly that Buchanan sent the homicidally furious Wilson to Gatsby's house, knowing that he would probably kill Gatsby. Nick finally prefers not to meet Tom again and only grudgingly shakes hands with him.

Daisy Buchanan, even more than her husband, is crucial to the meaning of the novel. Gatsby worships her, quite literally, as he stares across the water at the green light on her dock. His whole illicit career is an attempt to recapture Daisy. Yet from the beginning Nick finds her fraudulent. She tells him she finds life meaningless, not out of any real feeling, but because she thinks she is speaking what is currently in fashion. He is carried along by her beautiful, hypnotic voice, but when she finishes, he feels that she has cheated him. Daisy has not communicated. She has only performed. Later Nick says she dislikes Gatsby's parties because they are an "emotion" rather than a "gesture." It is doubtful that she would ever have confronted her husband with her love for Gatsby if Gatsby had not insisted on it. After she has rejected Gatsby for her husband, she makes no effort to save him when his life is in danger. She ignores his death and his funeral.

Nick sees all this and condemns it morally. "They were careless people, Tom and Daisy" (187). It would seem that Nick's analytical intelligence has saved him from the trap in which the unsophisticated Gatsby has been destroyed. But to read *The Great Gatsby* this way is to miss the full implications of Nick's personality—of the point of view from which the story has been told. He has, of course, escaped this trap, but he is caught in another; he has nothing left but desolation and despair. He has become the perfect person to tell Gatsby's story and to produce the mood, tone, and dimensions Fitzgerald wishes it to have. For the story is much more than a disillusionment with the pursuit of a rich girl or with the admiration of a monied class. The disillusionment is with contemporary American culture and in a sense with modern Western civilization. Perhaps the disillusionment is even cosmic.

Fitzgerald's world view in *The Great Gatsby* is, in part at least, of a piece with the spirit of the United States in the 1920s—a strange mixture of cynicism and outraged idealism, of despair and hysterical vitality. The primary reason was that the United States had just emerged from World War I, a war that had come as a surprise to most people. For the preceding two generations there had been a feeling that civilization was at last outgrowing war. Soon there would be no more wars. At the same time poets and philosophers yearned for the nobility and self-sacrifice that they believed war produced.

This war caused staggering loss of life throughout Europe as the first major war to be fought with poison gas and machine guns, and the losses seemed to lead to no conclusions but further losses. It was a grisly, pointless carnage that had no relation to the romantic conceptions of war common before the war began. The final reaction of the general public in the Allied countries was total revulsion. The reaction in defeated Germany, unfortunately, was homicidal desire for revenge.

But the case of the United States was somewhat different. When the war began in 1914, the United States determined to keep out, but by 1916 sympathy in this country was pro-Ally. German submarine warfare and reports of German atrocities (both true and false) left the American public enraged, but still in favor of neutrality. In 1916 Woodrow Wilson ran for his second term as president with the slogan "He kept us out of war." Only a few months after his reelection, the country, led by Wilson, plunged enthusiastically into the war.

After the war was over there was a general feeling that the nation had been tricked—that Wilson had deliberately misled the country. (Most historians today would agree that this is not so. Events in early 1917 made American involvement almost inevitable.) But Wilson had used slogans such as "Make the world safe for democracy" and "The war to end all wars." The peace settlement bore no resemblance to Wilson's promises. Historians who looked at it immediately predicted World War II. The United States even refused to join Wilson's League of Nations.

The reaction of most Americans to this situation was understandably cynical. Many intellectuals held the conviction that the hypocritical false idealism and loose thinking of an older generation had caused the war. But with the cynicism came great arrogance and great energy. The United States for the first time had settled a conflict among the major powers of the world. The country had lost many young men, but unlike European nations it had not depleted the manpower of a whole generation. European economies were in ruins. The United States had grown wealthier during the war and after a brief depression was off on the greatest economic expansion in its history.

Average Americans at this time were opposed to war and to any further involvement with Europe. They were willing to experiment with new sexual freedom and to drink bootleg liquor, but politically they opposed any sort of governmental activity that might limit business freedom. When President Coolidge told them that the business of the country was business, they agreed wholeheartedly. For most Americans at this time getting rich seemed the natural purpose of life.

Yet, in the excitement of all this business-oriented vitality, many Americans, especially the young and the educated, shared with many Europeans a belief that Western civilization was at an end. The war had shattered the smug Victorian belief that civilization was constantly progressing. Governments whose existence had been taken for granted for centuries—in Germany, in Austria, and in Russia—were now gone. On the left the communists believed that the war was the last desperate battle of capitalists over markets, and that capitalist economies and governments would now collapse. It looked for a while as though they were right. For the first time, a major world power, Russia, was controlled by communists. There were unsuccessful socialist revolutions in Germany and in Italy, and the English lived in fear of one. In the United States there were paralyzing strikes and a series of bombings. Federal authorities responded with mass arrests and deportations.

On the right, the German thinker Oswald Spengler argued in *The Decline of the West* (1918–1922) that cultures had an approximate life span of one thousand years and that Western culture, which began in the tenth century A.D., was now dying. Spengler believed that while the forms of government and social structure might survive this death, the values of the culture ceased to provide meaning for the lives of the people. The decadent West was concerned primarily with money and was falling under the control of the financially successful.

Another conservative thinker of the 1920s (in attitude, not, certainly, in poetic technique) was T. S. Eliot, whose *The Wasteland* (1922) became the most influential poem in English of the decade. Eliot, who was going through agonizing spiritual and emotional struggles when this poem was written, announced in 1929 that he had become a member of the Church of England and a royalist in politics. The theme of *The Wasteland* is the spiritual sterility of modern life, symbolized by images of desert, dust, rock, and decay, in a world waiting for rain that may or may not come. The rain is a deliberately ambiguous symbol that seems to stand for life, fertility, spiritual fulfillment, and salvation, but may also at the same time somehow be menacing, since it is sometimes associated with death.

Both Eliot and Spengler had a profound influence on Fitzgerald. Fitzgerald admired Eliot greatly and sent him a copy of *The Great Gatsby*. Eliot responded by saying that he thought the book was "the first step that American fiction has taken since Henry James." Eliot's approval may have been based partially on the fact that the novel is saturated with symbols and images from *The Wasteland*.

Spengler's influence was perhaps as strong as Eliot's. In 1940 Fitzgerald claimed to have read Spengler while writing *The Great Gatsby* and to have been permanently affected by him. About this early reading, however, he was mistaken. *The Decline of the West* was not translated into English until 1926, after *The Great Gatsby* was published, and Fitzgerald did not read German. The least attractive explanation for this discrepancy is that Fitzgerald realized that his novel could be taken as Spenglerian and decided to claim that the resemblance was intentional. The more likely explanation is that Fitzgerald read descriptions and analyses of Spengler's work in magazines, and later remembered incorrectly that he read Spengler before he actually did.

But undoubtedly Fitzgerald became a believer in Spengler's theories. In *The Love of the Last Tycoon*, the novel he left uncompleted at the time of his death in 1940, the heroine, Kathleen Moore, has been educated by her lover so that she could cap off her education by reading Spengler. Fitzgerald thought Spengler accurately explained the international situation at the beginning of World War II. Spengler believed that German militarism would play a dominant role in the last stages of Western civilization. Fitzgerald died expecting that the Nazis would easily conquer a decadent England and France and that the United States would fight the Germans in South America.

If *The Great Gatsby* is filled with symbols and images from *The Wasteland*, it also has symbols and images that are deeply compatible with *The Decline of the West*. What these works have in common is the belief that life in modern Western civilization has become meaningless. There are no genuine spiritual values remaining. In *The Great Gatsby* one of the finest values of Western culture, the American Dream, has lost its meaning. The American Dream promised the deepest and richest self-fulfillment for those who would make the most of their natural abilities. It was, of course, partly about money and comfort, but it was also about achievement and dignity. All that is left of it in Fitzgerald's novel is a crude pursuit of wealth and the superficial glamor that wealth provides. Those who have wealth, like the Buchanans, are shallow, empty, bored, unhappy people. Gatsby's tragedy is that his vague yearning for greatness has taken the only form available to him—a passion for the world of Daisy Buchanan.

Fitzgerald repeatedly draws analogies between Gatsby's world and the world of *The Wasteland*. The novel is pervaded by Eliot's principal images of spiritual sterility—a land which has become a desert through lack of rain, and a rain which may bring fertility and spiritual salvation, but may also, as a deluge of sensuality, bring death.

From the very beginning Fitzgerald uses images of dust, dryness, and desert. When Nick first mentions Gatsby, he talks of the "foul dust" that "floated in the wake of his dreams" (6). The area between West Egg and New York City where George Wilson's gas station is located is called a "valley of ashes." Over it appears a pair of huge pale eyes on the abandoned billboard of Doctor Eckleburg, an optometrist. These dead eyes of failed commercialism become a kind of God figure for the valley of ashes, the wasteland of the modern world. After Wilson has discovered his wife's infidelity and after she has been killed by a hit and run driver, he says while staring at the billboard, "God sees everything." His friend Michaelis replies, "That's an advertisement" (167). The eyes are the failed dead god of a wasteland, a delusion of spirituality.

The rain, too, is used symbolically. The rain falls heavily when Gatsby and Daisy meet for the first time in five years. Is this love and a kind of fertility, or a warning of death? Or, in light of what happens later, is it both? The rain falls steadily at Gatsby's funeral, where someone says, "Blessed are the dead that the rain falls on" (183). Fitzgerald lets the reader decide how much consolation this is meant to be.

The allusions to time in *The Great Gatsby*, like the wasteland images, bear out the hopelessness of Gatsby's dream and are probably deliberately Spenglerian. For a believer in Spengler's theories, inhabitants of modern Western civilization are trapped in time. They live in an age where no real creativity is possible, where there can be no renewal of spiritual vitality. No individual effort can change that. Gatsby's whole purpose is to repeat the past—to get back to some state of perfect love with Daisy. He refuses to believe that he cannot repeat the past. Symbolically, Gatsby nearly knocks over a clock during the awkwardness of his reunion with Daisy. When Nick recollects the grotesque people who came to Gatsby's parties and the ominous fates of some of them, he remarks that he has written their names on an old railway timetable.

The most painful thing that Gatsby learns in his confrontation with Tom Buchanan is that "you can't go home again," to borrow a phrase from Fitzgerald's contemporary fellow novelist Thomas Wolfe, because home is not there any more. What was once home has now changed into something else. Daisy cannot say she never loved her husband, as much antagonism as she may feel toward him. She has been married to a physically vital, sexually attractive man. She has had a child by him. As her husband says, there are experiences between him and Daisy that Gatsby will never know about.

Gatsby's inability to repeat the past is much more than the failure of an experience in romantic love, because for Gatsby that love is the essence of his powerful desire for a vaguely defined, self-fulfilling greatness. Gatsby's version of the American Dream is specific about only two things: money and Daisy. The dream is misguided, and it fails. His pathetic belief that if he can only reconstruct some point in the past everything will be all right reflects modern man's continuing search for meaning in a culture that no longer has meaning. Through Gatsby's experience Fitzgerald is describing what the American Dream has become in his time. The American Dream, one of the last and finest fruits of Western culture, has become dead (and deadly) materialism.

The last paragraphs of the novel reveal the final effect of Gatsby's experience on Nick, the cool, moral, intelligent observer who is disillusioned with everything Gatsby pursued, but is deeply sympathetic to Gatsby. Pondering near Gatsby's house, he sees the land as it appeared to the first European explorers when the trees "had once pandered in whispers to the last and greatest of all human dreams" (189). But if the dream ever had any substance, it is now over. Gatsby did not know that his dream was "already behind him." Nick talks about everyone, not just Gatsby, when he says we "are borne back ceaselessly into the past" (189).

Fitzgerald, through the voice of Nick, gives the novel a further dimension when he says that man, looking on the unexplored continent, was "face to face for the last time in history with something commensurate to his capacity for wonder" (189). Fitzgerald may or may not have had Spengler in mind when he wrote this passage. Spengler believed that each culture can be represented by a geometric figure and saw Western culture as a straight line going off into infinity. He called Western culture "Faustian," referring to the German poet Goethe's Faust, who is constantly searching and striving, always pushing beyond the limits of human experience. Gatsby is a Faustian man who has found nothing in his experience to match his longings. Nick, Gatsby's counterpart—the observer who tells Gatsby's story—has not been destroyed by his own efforts, as Gatsby has, but he is alone in a wasteland with no dreams and no hopes. This vision of despair may or may not come directly from Spengler. Certainly the larger issue it raises is universal: Can anything in real human experience live up to human hopes and human imagination? Are any of us, with our dreams, really very different from Gatsby?

STUDY QUESTIONS

1. This literary analysis sees Nick as someone of high moral character. Are there things in the story that would lead you to take exception to this? If so, what?

2. Analyze the character of one of the following. What do you think this person contributes to the novel?

    A. George Wilson

    B. Myrtle Wilson

    C. Jordan Baker

    D. Meyer Wolfsheim

    E. Owl Eyes

    F. Klipspringer

    G. Henry Gatz

3. The 1940s movie version of the novel begins with middle-aged Nick Carraway and Jordan Baker returning to Gatsby's grave. You learn that they have married. What events in the novel make this marriage highly improbable? How would the introduction of such a marriage affect the theme of the novel? Explain.

4. How would the novel be different if narrated by one of the following?

    A. Gatsby

    B. Daisy

    C. Tom

    D. George Wilson

    E. Owl Eyes

TOPICS FOR WRITTEN OR ORAL EXPLORATION

1. Read *This Side of Paradise* and compare it to *The Great Gatsby*. Are there ways in which one is superior to the other? Explain.

2. Read *Tender Is the Night* and compare and contrast it with *The Great Gatsby*. Are there ways in which one is superior to the other? Explain.

3. Write a brief play about the hotel scene in which you try to capture the same feeling the scene has in the novel. This is something that may be acted out in class.

4. *The Great Gatsby* deals with actions that are morally wrong, including adultery and criminal activity. Suppose you have met someone who disapproves of the novel because it deals with these subjects. Explain

how you would convince this person that he or she is mistaken in thinking that the novel is improper.

5. The analysis you have just read states that everything in *The Great Gatsby* contributes to the overall effect of the novel. A number of events, images, and symbols are repeated at crucial points in the novel. Trace the appearances of one of the following and explain their significance.

    A. The phone conversations

    B. Cars and careless driving

    C. Eyes in addition to Doctor Eckleburg's

    D. Music

    E. Significant colors

    F. The party scenes

6. Read *The Wasteland* and identify allusions to it, other than the ones already mentioned, in *The Great Gatsby*. Pay special attention to the trip Nick and Gatsby make to New York City in Chapter 4.

7. Read Fitzgerald's story "The Diamond as Big as the Ritz" and compare its theme to that of *The Great Gatsby*. Pay special attention to the conclusions of both works.

8. Read Herman Melville's story "Bartleby the Scrivener." Notice how the narrator is affected by events he describes. Compare and contrast his final state of mind with that of Nick Carraway.

SUGGESTIONS FOR FURTHER READING

A great many books analyze *The Great Gatsby*. The following list does not include them all, but it will give you a start:

Berman, Donald. *"The Great Gatsby" and Modern Times*. Urbana: University of Illinois Press, 1994.

Cross, K.G.W. *Scott Fitzgerald*. London: Oliver and Boyd, 1964.

Henderson, Jack. *"This Side of Paradise" as a Bildungsroman*. New York: Peter Lang, 1993.

Lehan, Richard. *F. Scott Fitzgerald and the Craft of Fiction*. Carbondale: Southern Illinois University Press, 1966.

Miller, James E., Jr. *The Fictional Technique of Scott Fitzgerald*. The Hague: Martinus Wijhoff, 1957.

Piper, Henry Dan. *F. Scott Fitzgerald: A Critical Portrait*. New York: Holt, Rinehart and Winston, 1964.

Sklar, Robert. *F. Scott Fitzgerald: The Last Laocoön*. New York: Oxford
    University Press, 1967.
Weston, Elizabeth A. *The International Theme in F. Scott Fitzgerald's
    Literature*. New York: Peter Lang, 1995.

2

The Great Gatsby and F. Scott Fitzgerald: Intertwining of Life and Work

Much more than most writers, Fitzgerald was a public figure. The press of the 1920s was very aware of his lifestyle—a lifestyle that seemed daring and glamorously desirable to thousands of envious readers. Fitzgerald exploited this image in more than one way. Popular magazines often published articles by and about him; and more than most writers, he based a good deal of his fiction on his own personal experiences. During his lifetime it was not always easy to tell when his life furnished material for his fiction and when his fiction furnished material for his life; now, more than fifty years after his death, it is more difficult than ever.

Because of this intertwining of his life and his work, biographical information contributes to an understanding of *The Great Gatsby*. But at this point it is well to be cautious. Although many writers have used biographical material in their fiction, it is unlikely that any major writer created fiction solely for the purpose of writing about his life. Almost any perceptive reader will see that Fitzgerald, either consciously or unconsciously, brought his internal conflicts into his fiction. But this is not to say that his fiction does not also have a meaning entirely independent of his personal life. The literary analysis of *The Great Gatsby* in Chapter 1 of this book, for example, is entirely free of biographical interpretation. In this chapter we will examine the life that provided some of the raw material for the fiction.

Born in St. Paul, Minnesota, in 1896, Fitzgerald was the son of a salesman for Procter & Gamble whose career was ruined when he lost his job in 1908. The family, which had been living in New York State, returned to St. Paul. Although Fitzgerald's father ran a wholesale grocery business, the family now depended on money from his mother's relatives. His father's relatives had culture and tradition, but the socially inferior relatives on his mother's side had money. Each side looked down on the other. Fitzgerald was often deeply embarrassed by his mother, who was often talked about in St. Paul for her awkward and eccentric behavior.

This conflict between culture and wealth in his background made Fitzgerald very conscious both of money and of social standing, and it also made him very uncertain of his own social position. All his life he pursued conventional status symbols, yet a part of his mind stood apart and viewed these status symbols coldly and cynically. Be aware of these conflicting attitudes when you observe the interactions of Jay Gatsby the social climber, Tom Buchanan the wealthy businessman, and Nick Carraway the young man of culture and family.

Fitzgerald attended Newman, a Roman Catholic preparatory school. Like many of its graduates, he went on to Princeton, enrolling in 1913. He was able to afford this exclusive school because he inherited money from his maternal grandmother. Today, about half of American high school graduates receive some higher education, but as late as 1940 only 5 percent of the population attended college. Of these only a handful attended elite Ivy League universities like Harvard, Yale, and Princeton, or women's colleges of high standing like Vassar and Smith. In 1913 these schools heavily favored applicants from socially prominent families, especially families with money. This is not to say that the academic standards of the time were not high, of course.

Although Fitzgerald's own background was socially respectable, it was no match for the backgrounds of many of his classmates. As soon as he arrived he tried to distinguish himself by playing football. At that time to be a gentleman athlete at a famous university was the essence of glamor. His football career lasted one day. He next attempted to distinguish himself by concentrating on his writing, especially on musical comedies and on other pieces for the

Triangle Club, a powerful undergraduate literary society. He was very successful as a writer and as a social figure, and he formed lifelong friendships with critic Edmund Wilson and poet John Peale Bishop. But academically he was in constant trouble, and his dissipation, especially his heavy drinking, undermined his health. He left college during his junior year, claiming he had tuberculosis; in fact, he was expecting to flunk out if he completed the year. Later in life he actually did contract tuberculosis, and the bad academic record bothered him as long as he lived. He returned to the university the next fall, but never graduated.

By this time, the United States had entered World War I, and Fitzgerald embarked upon a career as a frighteningly incompetent army officer. During officers' training classes he sat in the rear of the classroom writing the first draft of his first novel, which he then called "The Romantic Egotist." As a result he learned practically nothing about military regulations. He committed blunders, and other trainees played practical jokes on him. Once they talked him into forcing a conscientious objector in his outfit to drill at gunpoint immediately after they had been taught that to do so was an offense for which an officer could be court-martialed. Fortunately for him and for the army, the war ended before he saw combat.

So far his love life had been as unsuccessful as his army life and college life. While in college he spent two years pursuing Ginevra King, who kept many suitors dangling. She never seemed to have taken Fitzgerald seriously, and married someone else. While stationed in Montgomery, Alabama, he fell in love with the very popular, flirtatious Zelda Sayre, the daughter of a prominent but highly mentally and emotionally unstable family.

This time his love was returned, and Fitzgerald, with no financial prospects, looked about for some way to support his fiancée. "The Romantic Egotist," written largely while he sat in his army training classes, was praised by Scribner's but rejected. He took a job with a New York advertising firm, which he quit when Zelda ran out of patience and broke their engagement. He returned to St. Paul and revised his first novel. It became *This Side of Paradise*, which was accepted for publication by Scribner's. This was the major turning point of his life.

This first book sold 20,000 copies in its first week and 49,000 by the end of 1921. *This Side of Paradise* has much in common with the novels that followed it. It expressed the new mood of the

United States in the years immediately following World War I—a mood that Fitzgerald helped to develop in his fiction at the same time that he expressed it in his own life. The hero, Amory Blaine, an aristocratic, rather pampered young man, loses his illusions as he makes a poor record at Princeton in spite of his brilliance, loses classmates in World War I, loses the girl he loves (and who loves him) to a wealthy suitor, and then finds that he has lost what little remained of his inherited money and must now seek the sort of mediocre employment for which he is fitted. Finally he says, "I know myself, but that is all." The similarity between Fitzgerald's situation and that of Amory Blaine is obvious.

This Side of Paradise owes much of its appeal to the genteel, mellow Princeton atmosphere it evokes, and to the urbane, witty cynicism of Amory and his friends. But it owes more of its appeal to the public's fascination with the new free morality of its young men and women. The girl Amory loses is an early example of the glamorous flappers of the 1920s, and she is modeled closely on Zelda Sayre. Some of Zelda's conversations and even some of her writing went into this novel.

Fitzgerald did not invent the term *flapper*, but more than any other single writer he popularized it when he created its first literary expression. Flappers seized personal freedom for themselves; earlier American women could not have imagined such behavior being socially acceptable. These young women asserted their right to smoke and drink. They often danced the daring new dances of the twenties all night and engaged in personal behavior that shocked an older generation. They dispensed with chaperones, dated widely, flirted with many men, and shamelessly allowed themselves to be kissed. As far as actual sexual behavior goes, Alfred Kinsey, based on surveys made in the 1950s, found that women coming to maturity right after World War I behaved more like women of the 1950s than women only slightly older than themselves.

Zelda Sayre became a model for many of Fitzgerald's heroines. Pursued by men from her mid-teens on, she flirted with her admirers and treated them heartlessly. Like Fitzgerald's heroines, she was selfish and whimsical. She loved to shock with mildly sexual exhibitionism. She was very attractive—to many people, she was irresistible. Unlike most of Fitzgerald's flappers, at least as he specifically describes them, Zelda had been sexually active since she was fifteen, unusual behavior for a girl of her social background in the 1920s. Even considering the rapid changes in acceptable behavior that were taking place during the period, Zelda Sayre was liberated sexually.

On April 3, 1920, Scott and Zelda were married. Their daughter Scottie, their only child, was born on October 26, 1921. Like most people of his generation, Fitzgerald had been brought up with very strict rules of sexual behavior, and he always remained uneasy about Zelda's past and about his own premarital relations with her. His attitudes toward the heroines he created are very mixed. They are often selfish and unaware of the consequences of their behavior. Yet these women are irresistibly attractive. They often come to be the only meaning in men's lives. At the same time, Fitzgerald feels great sympathy for the economic plight of his heroines, as Sarah Beebe Fryer points out in *Fitzgerald's New Women*. Unlike women today, they have little ability to support themselves and have few options other than to marry men who can support them. Still, the fact remains that Fitzgerald would always know that Zelda could not or would not marry him until he had financial prospects.

In the early years of their marriage Scott and Zelda were very much public figures, especially in the night life of New York City. They behaved like Fitzgerald's fictional characters (a bit more wild than most of them, if anything), and some of this uninhibited behavior appeared in his fiction. They attended and gave a great many parties featuring illegal alcohol, and they frequented the speakeasies (illegal drinking places) of the Prohibition era. They wrecked a car in a park and went for midnight swims in park ponds. While Zelda cheered him on, Fitzgerald assaulted the bouncer in a speakeasy and was soundly beaten up. They were ejected from theaters for being disruptive, and they were asked to leave one rented residence after another because of their lifestyle. This behavior made them a favorite subject of the tabloids, and the publicity helped to sell Fitzgerald's stories and to make him the most highly paid magazine fiction writer of the twenties. The public came to expect him to write the kind of stories it associated with his life.

Many people feel that Zelda both inspired and destroyed Fitzgerald. Much of her behavior and many of her qualities went into his heroines, and so did some of her actual language and writing. Certainly she was a major part of his public image. Yet she was extravagant, much more so than her extravagant husband. He wanted to write serious novels, but instead kept turning out mediocre stories for quick money. Zelda lured him away from his writing to parties. Perhaps he resented her (or even hated her) as much as he loved her.

Zelda served as the model for Gloria Gilbert, the heroine of Fitzgerald's second novel, *The Beautiful and Damned* (1922). Gloria is a more fully developed character than Rosalind Connage, the Zelda-figure of *This Side of Paradise*, but it is open to question whether Gloria is meant to be more sympathetic. Rosalind Connage loves Amory Blaine but marries someone else because Blaine is unable to support her in any style, let alone the style to which she is accustomed. Gloria Gilbert loves Anthony Patch, the man she marries, but she is extremely spoiled and willful. They live on his inheritance, but from the first they overspend, constantly depleting the principal. At first she shares in his dissipations and extravagances, but as he becomes alcoholic, she tries to restrain him. As their financial plight becomes serious, she tries in her helpless way to point him toward some way of making money. After his final collapse she becomes his caretaker. They now live on a fortune inherited from his grandfather, which they had nearly lost in a long court battle. She is not a very strong person, and she shows only a little of Rosalind Connage's wit and intelligence.

The life the Fitzgeralds lived from 1920 to 1924 was quite a bit like the life lived by Anthony and Gloria Patch. One of the chief differences between Fitzgerald and Anthony Patch was that Fitzgerald had a great talent that enabled him to make money. Perhaps Anthony Patch was what Fitzgerald was afraid he might become. Another important difference was that Anthony Patch has an affair, which is one of the things that causes his breakdown. Fitzgerald was then faithful to his wife. Zelda flirted constantly, but for the time being she was faithful to him.

In 1924 Fitzgerald was living on the Riviera, part of the American expatriate community in France. While he was working on his next novel, *The Great Gatsby*, he underwent a cataclysmic experience that nearly destroyed his marriage. Zelda had been having an affair with Édouard Jozan, a young French military officer. She told Fitzgerald she wanted a divorce, but Jozan was unwilling to marry her. She took an overdose of sleeping pills, and Fitzgerald spent the night trying to save her life by desperately walking her to keep her awake. At this time he wanted his marriage to survive, but his life with Zelda would never be the same.

Many of the conflicts of these years appear in *The Great Gatsby*. The novel differs from the first two in that it is less directly autobiographical. The lives of Amory Blaine and Anthony Patch are roughly parallel to Fitzgerald's own. But although no one in *The Great Gatsby* closely resembles Fitzgerald, many of the elements of his life are here. The New York night life so familiar to the readers of the tabloids, the preoccupation with money at all levels of society, Gatsby's fixation on a beautiful woman, and the hopeless marital difficulties depicted with such clear precision are autobiographical aspects of this novel, and they are among the forces that make reading it an unforgettable experience.

Three consecutive Fitzgerald novels deal with adultery. Anthony Patch's collapse is partially caused by his adultery. In *Tender Is the Night*, the novel following *The Great Gatsby*, the hero, Dick Diver, shows the first signs of decay when he has an extramarital affair. *The Great Gatsby* is, among other things, a story of adultery. The theme had come to preoccupy Fitzgerald in *The Beautiful and Damned* before Zelda's adultery, and it is treated most powerfully in *The Great Gatsby*, the novel he was writing when her adultery occurred.

Although most critics realized how good *The Great Gatsby* is, it sold only 25,000 copies—only 5,000 more copies than the first week's sales of *This Side of Paradise*—not nearly enough to solve Fitzgerald's financial problems. Between 1920 and 1925 Fitzgerald had published three novels, many short stories, and a play. He did not publish another novel until 1934, when *Tender Is the Night* appeared.

From the late 1920s until his death in 1940, Fitzgerald suffered one misfortune after another. He worked and reworked *Tender Is the Night*, making fundamental changes in the plot and putting in and taking out characters. Most of the critics Fitzgerald valued praised it, and he was convinced that it was his best book. He was terribly disappointed in the total sale of only 13,000 copies. His days of financial prosperity were now over. The prices magazines paid for his stories had declined sharply, and sometimes magazines were not willing to take them at all.

In his personal life, too, one thing after another went wrong. Zelda suffered a mental breakdown in 1930 and was diagnosed as schizophrenic. (The *Random House Dictionary* defines this disease as "a severe mental disorder characterized by some, but not necessarily all, of the following features: emotional blunting, intellectual deterioration, social isolation, disorganized speech and behavior, delusions, and hallucinations.") She seemed to recover, but collapsed again. Fitzgerald knew this meant that she would be in and out of mental institutions for the rest of her life. He was now clearly an alcoholic. He had little control over his drinking once he started, and at times went on binges. He developed tuberculosis, and his nervous condition was so bad that he could sleep only by taking very strong medication. In the morning he needed other strong medications to bring him around. Finally he developed the heart condition that killed him.

Many critics in the 1930s preferred novels and plays with obvious social and economic messages, often with a Marxian slant. On the part of both critics and the reading public there was a growing interest in literature about slums, racial minorities, and the culturally primitive. Highly popular works from this period include Clifford Odet's play *Waiting For Lefty* (1935), in which oppressed workers decide to strike, and John Steinbeck's novella *Of Mice and Men* (1937), a story about migrant workers who plan unsuccessfully to establish their own home.

Fitzgerald paid a price writers sometimes pay for early success. As long as he lived, he was identified with his early work in the public mind. The Jazz Age that he had helped to create was over. To most people, he was part of that age—a bygone era.

In 1937 he went to Hollywood, where he was at first paid $1,000 a week, at that time a splendid salary. He studied film writing carefully and worked hard, but, like many good novelists, he had little success as a screenwriter. Like many others, though, Fitzgerald made good money. Hollywood then was amazingly inefficient. The British humorous writer P. G. Wodehouse, for example, once was paid $104,000 Depression dollars for a year's work, and he said that by the end of the year he had been given only three very minor assignments, one of which, as far as he knew, was never used.

Fitzgerald began work on a Hollywood novel, which he intended to call *The Love of the Last Tycoon*, loosely based on the career of Irving Thalberg, a brilliant producer whom Fitzgerald greatly admired. He died before completing it, but the published fragment has impressed most critics as very fine work. Interest in his work remained slight throughout the 1940s, but the Fitzgerald revival, which began with Budd Schulberg's novel *The Disenchanted* (1950), a thinly disguised account of Fitzgerald's Hollywood period, and Arthur Mizener's biography of Fitzgerald, *The Far Side of Paradise* (1951), continues to this day. Fitzgerald is now generally regarded as one of his country's greatest novelists.

CRITICISM OF FITZGERALD'S EARLY WORK

A June 1920 article in *Current Opinion* on young writers contains some early critical reactions to *This Side of Paradise*. The article describes Fitzgerald as "a sensation at twenty-three" and goes on to say that his "first novel has awakened wide comment. He has been accepted by *Scribner's* and the *Saturday Evening Post*. The dangers of an early success, it is said, outnumber its rewards" (825).

FROM "OUR NEW NOVELISTS OF THE 'EARLY TWENTIES' "
(Current Opinion, June 1920, pp. 824–25)

Youth is undoubtedly having its day in literature . . . two young novelists . . . have won recently a discriminating welcome from the critics. One of these is F. Scott Fitzgerald, whose novel, "This Side of Paradise" (Scribner), fired with the enthusiasm of youth, deals with undergraduate days at Princeton. The other is Robert Nathan, whose "Peter Kindred" (Duffield) is a semi-autobiographic account of the making of a Harvard graduate. As expressions of what one may term the "1920 class" of American novelists, both these works of fiction have been hailed as significant.

F. Scott Fitzgerald, we are informed by the N.Y. *Evening Sun*, has, at the age of 23, written a novel in "the very contemporary accent of youth, seen in the light of a wisdom he has somehow managed to steal from an overtaken middle age." It is called "a novel about flappers for philosophers," and, when the manuscript came to the office of the publishers, "keep in a cool, dry place" was written on it. The *Evening Post* says of this new arrival in American fiction:

"Through him our youngest adult generation of the class socially preferred and our educational system's most recent output of the class endowed with brains and temperament give us self portraits done with a critical eye and a sure hand. Mr. Fitzgerald's subject, Amory Blaine, is a member of both these classes. While writing piecemeal the record of Amory's progress, compiling a kind of loose scrap-book of the history of the case, he affords us much inside knowledge of the atmosphere that surrounds a luxurious twentieth century childhood in the Middle West, a very high caste 'prep' school in the East, the corresponding caste among the students of a leading university, and at least one 'younger set' of that hard, competitive, conspicuous element of present-day society in New York which rules itself altogether by the gold standard.

"But quickly, lest the foregoing seem to indicate a dreary novel by a top-heavy young sociological realist, let it be added that 'This Side of Paradise' is a very enlivening book indeed, a book really brilliant and glamorous, making as agreeable reading as could be asked. It has a profusion of incidental appetizing features.

"There are clever things, keen and searching things, amusing young and mistaken things, beautiful things and pretty things—these last named including some pleasant poems—and truly inspired and elevated things, an astonishing abundance of each in 'This Side of Paradise.' You could call it the youthful Byronism that is normal in a man of the author's type, working out through a well-furnished intellect of unusual critical force."

There is something in this beginning, says the critic of the *Nation*, that recalls a fluttering banner and a bugle at dawn:

"He is still largely absorbed by mere form and mere mood—the literary passions of youth. No one will object to his telling his story through impressionistic episodes, letters, poems, dramatic interludes. But these matters of external method have less importance than he thinks today. Nor are they nearly so insurgent. Insurgency is in the mind and builds its form from within outward. But Mr. Fitzgerald's mind is still hovering uncertainly on the shore of new seas of thought. It is—to risk a bull—rather afraid of wetting its feet. So, too, with his moods. He has not yet reached any thought or perception that is absolutely his own.

"His story, as one would expect, is in the deeper sense if not in outer circumstances, autobiographical. His gifts have an unmistakable amplitude and much in his book is brave and beautiful."

The critic of the N.Y. *Sun* delights in the youthful "cheekiness" of this first novel:

"It is the first self-conscious and self-critical offering of the exceptionally 'brilliant' contingent among the American youth whom 1917 overtook in college. You could think of it as the New Youth, more differentiated by the war than even the new Middle Age has realized, talking about itself in public exuberantly and yet with a certain sobriety and conviction that youth never had before; taking itself very seriously and deprecating the seriousness; unable (as a great dramatist said of the nonage of another) to keep its brains quiet, but worth a hearing even in the absurdest flights of their loquacity."

Heywood Broun, who indulges in somewhat solipsistic book-reviews in the N.Y. *Tribune*, confesses that "This Side of Paradise" makes him feel very old. "Daisy Ashford is hardly more naive. There is a certain confusion arising from the fact that, in spite of the generally callow quality of the author's point of view, he is intent on putting himself over as a cynical and searching philosopher. The resulting strain is sometimes terrific."

HEYWOOD BROUN

Heywood Broun, who is quoted at the conclusion of the previous article, was one of the most influential dissenters to the favorable reception of *This Side of Paradise*. The public generally found the novel shocking and daring, and speculated that Fitzgerald's personal life must match his fiction. The disillusionment of its characters shocked readers at least as much as their behavior.

But Broun found the whole performance rather boring. Young men of college age had always gone through disillusionment, he said. Their late adolescent maunderings were hardly a subject for good fiction. Fitzgerald was hurt badly by the attack; he invited Broun to lunch and told him that it was too bad that Broun had reached the age of thirty without accomplishing anything. Fitzgerald's comment was probably right to the point. Envy of a very successful, very young novelist was probably a major factor in Broun's criticism. Broun then published the following interview with Fitzgerald by Carleton R. Davis, tacking on his own comment at the end.

FROM HEYWOOD BROUN, "BOOKS"
(New York Tribune, May 4, 1920)

Having from time to time set down our impression of F. Scott Fitzgerald who wrote "This Side of Paradise," it seems only fair to step aside and let Mr. Fitzgerald talk for himself, as he does in an interview by Carleton R. Davis, which is sent to us by Scribner's.

> With the distinct intention of taking Mr. Fitzgerald by surprise I ascended to the twenty-fifth floor of the Biltmore and knocked in the best waiter-manner at the door. On entering, my first impression was one of confusion—sort of rummage sale confusion. A young man was standing in the center of the room, twining an absent glance first at one side of the room and then at the other.
>
> "I'm looking for my hat," he said, dazedly. "How do you do? Come on in and sit down on the bed."
>
> The author of "This Side of Paradise" is sturdy, broad shouldered and just about medium height. He has blond hair, with the suggestion of a wave, and alert green eyes—mélange somewhat Nordic—

and good looking, too, which was disconcerting, as I had somehow expected a thin nose and spectacles.

We had preliminaries—but I will omit the preliminaries—they consisted in searching for things, cigarettes, a blue tie with white dots, an ash tray. But as he was obviously quite willing to talk and seemed quite receptive to my questions, we launched off directly on his ideas of literature.

"How long did it take to write your book?" I began.

"To write it—three months. To conceive it—three minutes. To collect the data in it—all my life. The idea of writing it occurred to me on the first of last July. It was a sort of a substitute form of dissipation."

"What are your plans now?" I asked him.

"I'll be darned if I know. The scope and depth and breadth of my writings lie in the laps of the gods. If knowledge comes naturally through interest, as Shaw learned his political economy or as Wells devoured modern science—why, that'll be slick. On study itself—that is, in 'reading up' a subject—I haven't anthill moving faith. Knowledge must cry out to be known—cry out that only I can know it, and then I'll swim in—in many things."

"Please be frank."

"Well, you know if you've read my book, I've swum in various seas of adolescent egotism. But what I meant was that if big things never grip me—well, it simply means I'm not cut out to be big. This conscious struggle to find bigness outside, to substitute bigness of theme for bigness of perception, to create an objective *Magnum Opus* such as 'The Ring and the Book'—well; all that's the antithesis of my literary aims.

"Another thing," he continued. "My idea is always to reach my generation. The wise writer, I think, writes for the youth of his own generation, the critics of the next, and the schoolmasters of ever afterward. Granted the ability to improve what he imitates in the way of style, to choose from his own interpretation of the experiences around him what constitutes material, and we get the first-water genius."

"Do you expect to be—to be—well, part of the great literary tradition?" I asked timidly.

He became excited. He smiled radiantly. I saw he had an answer to this.

"There's no great literary tradition," he burst out. "The wise literary son kills his own father."

After this he began enthusiastically on style.

"By style, I mean color," he said. "I want to be able to do anything with words, handle slashing, flaming description like Wells, and use the paradox with the clarity of Samuel Butler, [the] breadth of Bernard Shaw and the wit of Oscar Wilde. I want to do the wide sultry heavens of Conrad, the rolled-gold sundowns and crazy-quilt skies of Hichens and Kipling, as well as the pastel dawns and twilights of Chesterton. All that is by way of example. As a matter of fact, I am a professed literary thief, hot after the best methods of every writer in my generation."

• • •

Having heard Mr. Fitzgerald, we are not entirely minded to abandon our notion that he is a rather complacent, somewhat pretentious and altogether self-conscious young man.

THE WORLD'S WORK ON THIS SIDE OF PARADISE

The following brief entry is perhaps typical of the responses to the novel in what it notices: the book is highly controversial, and it sells. The photograph of Fitzgerald, taken soon after the publication of his first novel, accompanied the following comment.

FROM NOTICE OF *THIS SIDE OF PARADISE*
(*The World's Work*, June 1921, p. 192)

Written in a daring and iconoclastic spirit that reflects the youth of its author, Mr. Scott Fitzgerald's "This Side of Paradise" has been one of the most highly praised and bitterly criticized novels of recent years. The first printing was exhausted the day of publication. Already there have been eleven printings of the book.

Fitzgerald at the time of his successful first novel.

STUDY QUESTIONS

1. After reading a biography of Fitzgerald, decide to what extent Gatsby resembles Fitzgerald.

2. Read a Fitzgerald biography to decide how much Nick Carraway has in common with Fitzgerald.

3. How much does the love affair between Daisy and Gatsby have in common with Zelda's love affair with Édouard Jozan? What are the differences?

4. How much does Daisy have in common with Zelda? What are the differences between them?

5. Tom Buchanan's situation in the novel is much like Fitzgerald's in real life. Both wanted to hang on to wives who were in love with other men. Are there any similarities between Tom and Fitzgerald? What are some of the differences?

6. The parties in *The Great Gatsby* are somewhat like the parties Fitzgerald attended in real life. What is Fitzgerald's attitude toward the parties in the novel? How does he want the reader to feel about them?

7. Imagine F. Scott Fitzgerald being your age today. How would his life differ from the one which Fitzgerald lived?

8. Write a short play about an episode in Fitzgerald's life.

9. Note that the literary analysis in Chapter 1 does not rely on Fitzgerald's biography. Chapter 2 is an approach to the novel based on his life. If the biographical approach is taken too far, might it actually distort what the author is trying to say? Do you feel you know the novel better because you know something about the author's life? Defend your answer.

10. Based on Carleton Davis' interview, Broun characterizes Fitzgerald as "complacent" and "pretentious." Analyze the interview and give your own reactions to it. Could some of what Fitzgerald says actually be taken as an indication of humility? Do positive qualities of Fitzgerald come through in this interview? If so, what are they? Remember that the interview was released by Fitzgerald's publisher. Scribner's would not intentionally have released anything likely to damage one of their authors. If it had been up to you, would you have released the interview? Defend your answer.

11. What do you think Fitzgerald meant when he said, "The wise literary son kills his own father"? Do you think he is right?

TOPICS FOR WRITTEN OR ORAL EXPLORATION

1. After reading *This Side of Paradise, The Beautiful and Damned*, or *Tender Is the Night*, as well as *The Great Gatsby*, make one or more of these comparisons.

   1. Compare Jay Gatsby and Amory Blaine.
   2. Compare Jay Gatsby and Anthony Patch.
   3. Compare Jay Gatsby and Dick Diver.
   4. Compare Daisy Buchanan and Rosalind Connage.
   5. Compare Daisy Buchanan and Gloria Patch.
   6. Compare Daisy Buchanan and Nicole Diver.

2. Many modern novelists, including Fitzgerald, Ernest Hemingway, and Thomas Wolf, use incidents from their lives in their fiction. Would you rather read a novel based on an author's life or one that has little to do with his or her life? Explain why.

SUGGESTIONS FOR FURTHER READING

Ever since the publication of Arthur Mizener's biography of F. Scott Fitzgerald in 1951, there has been a steady stream of books about the author's life. While not comprehensive, this list is a good starting place.

Bruccoli, Matthew. *Some Sort of Epic Grandeur: A Life of Scott Fitzgerald*. New York: Harcourt Brace Jovanovich, 1981.

Donaldson, Scott. *Fool for Love: A Biography of F. Scott Fitzgerald*. New York: Delta, 1983.

Mayfield, Sara. *Exiles from Paradise: Scott and Zelda Fitzgerald*. New York: Delacorte Press, 1974.

Mellow, James. *Invented Lives: F. Scott and Zelda Fitzgerald*. Boston: Houghton Mifflin, 1984.

Meyers, Jeffrey. *Scott Fitzgerald: A Biography*. New York: HarperCollins, 1994. Meyers is the primary source for the biographical information in this chapter.

Mizener, Arthur. *The Far Side of Paradise: A Biography of F. Scott Fitzgerald*. 1951. Rev. ed. Boston: Houghton Mifflin, 1965.

Piper, Henry Dan. *F. Scott Fitzgerald: A Critical Portrait*. Carbondale: Southern Illinois University Press, 1965.

Turnbull, Andrew. *Scott Fitzgerald*. New York: Charles Scribner's Sons, 1962. Turnbull is the source for the information about Fitzgerald's military life in this chapter.

3

Why Be Honest? The Scandals of the 1920s

The Great Gatsby is a book about disillusionment with the American dream of success as that dream is misunderstood by Jay Gatsby, who sees no difference between his success as a criminal and legitimate forms of achievement. Fitzgerald emphasizes this theme by alluding to corruption in professional sports and to underworld figures for whom many Americans were coming to have a misplaced admiration.

· The American tendency not to respect the law, magnified many times over by Prohibition, made folk heroes of gangsters like Dutch Schultz and of nightclub hostesses like Texas Guinan. The mystery and glamor surrounding Gatsby and the hysterical wildness of his parties are a reflection of the underworld where these figures flourished. Gatsby's disillusionment and his fate show Fitzgerald's own disillusioned appraisal of that world.

Several events that affected Fitzgerald and the American public are discussed in this chapter, including the exposure of political corruption in the Harding administration and the shock the country felt when it learned of corruption in its most cherished sport, major league baseball. We will also look at some of the activities of organized crime.

Although organized crime—gambling, for instance—existed long before Gatsby's time, criminal activity increased greatly during

Prohibition. One of Gatsby's main criminal activities, of course, is bootlegging.

The Prohibition era began with the ratification of the Eighteenth Amendment to the Constitution in January 1919, which made it legal to forbid by law the selling of alcoholic drinks. With the passage of the Volstead Act in the same year, it became illegal to sell, manufacture, and transport alcohol. Prohibition ended in December 1933 with the passage of the Twenty-first Amendment to the Constitution, repealing the Eighteenth.

From the first, Prohibition was unenforceable. People tried almost everything to get alcohol. They made home brew and built their own stills. They smuggled liquor across United States borders. They obtained medical prescriptions for alcohol. But large-scale criminals became the most important suppliers. These "bootleggers" built breweries and brought in shiploads of liquor by sea and truckloads from Canada.

All over the United States speakeasies opened to supply illegal drinks to the public. (There are two common guesses about where this strange word comes from. First, a person would need to "speak easy"—rather than make a racket—so as not to call the attention of law enforcement officers to the place. Second, it may be related to the idea that it was quite "easy" to obtain illegal liquor—all one needed to do was "speak" at the door to get in. Another expression for a speakeasy was "blind pig," which dates back to the 1830s. To evade an earlier prohibition against selling liquor, men were invited to see a very unusual pig, a striped pig. When they got inside they found a model of a pig and a glass of hard liquor—the cost of this liquor was the cost of admission. The pig was a "blind pig" because the whole thing was secret, hidden.) In New York City alone hundreds of speakeasies appeared, most of them selling cheap and even dangerously contaminated liquor at high prices. The food served was usually bad, and the entertainment vulgar and of poor quality. Most of these places had understandings with local law enforcement officers and were not raided, but they were in some danger of occasional raids by federal agents.

The worst of the speakeasies were in danger from all of the authorities, and for very good reasons. These places were called "clip joints." Customers were sent there thinking they would get good liquor and sometimes access to prostitutes. They were served raw bad liquor, and if they could be gotten drunk enough, they were robbed and thrown out. If they did not get hopelessly drunk, they were accused of molesting hostesses or of refusing to pay for great quantities of liquor they had not ordered. They were threatened with beatings if they did not pay the money demanded, and if they resisted, they were usually beaten and robbed. When the police found a clip joint, they smashed everything in the place and beat up all the employees they could find. The lawbreakers were treated lawlessly.

Organized crime grew tremendously, and leading gangsters, like Wolfsheim and Gatsby in the novel, became wealthy. But their lives were in constant danger as they fought each other for territory and as they double-crossed each other. In addition to watching each other they had to watch out for law officers. On one hand, there seems to have been an unspoken understanding in some cases that when gangsters killed each other the police would not look too hard for the killers. On the other hand, when gangsters killed citizens who were not criminals themselves, the police would look hard for the killers, and when gangsters killed policemen the police would look very hard. Notice that in one important respect nightclub hostess Texas Guinan differs from most of the underworld figures discussed in this chapter. Unlike Herman Rosenthal, Arnold Rothstein, Larry Fay, Vincent Coll, and Dutch Schultz, she did not die a violent death. Another exception was Al Capone, whose mind was destroyed by syphilis while he was imprisoned in Alcatraz. Yet even Capone, possibly the most powerful man in Chicago, at times feared for his life.

The tense, ominous quality under the surface of *The Great Gatsby* reflects the danger of Gatsby's world. Notice the menacing touches to the descriptions of Gatsby and the nature of the rumors about him. Notice the descriptions of those who attend Gatsby's parties and the sense of doom in those descriptions. And notice too that in this novel corruption is everywhere and that men like Gatsby have great influence.

The corruption spread far beyond the world of the gangsters themselves, into sports, politics, and law enforcement. The death of Herman Rosenthal, a pre-Prohibition case discussed below, occurred because of the criminal involvement of New York policemen. The most blatant examples occurred in Chicago and nearby Cicero, Illinois, rather than in New York.

In 1924 Roger St. John, editor of the Cicero *Tribune*, ran articles about Capone's houses of prostitution. He was severely beaten by Capone's brother Ralph and by two other thugs while two policemen stood by and watched. When he left the hospital, he discovered that Capone had paid his bill. He then went to the police station to file charges, but found the police reluctant. They asked him to return. When he came back, he found Capone waiting for him. Capone tried his best to bribe St. John, but without success. Next, St. John found that Capone had bought a controlling interest in the Cicero *Tribune*, using one of his henchmen as a front man. Finally St. John gave up.

When the comedian Milton Berle performed in Chicago, Capone asked him to play at a Capone club. Berle at first refused, because his commitment to perform elsewhere left him without the necessary time. But after he agreed he was carried at high speed in an armored car through all the traffic lights. Among other prominent guests at his show was Chicago mayor Big Bill Thompson. Capone, by the way, was a very heavy contributor to Thompson's campaign fund.

Incidents like these made the average person very cynical about politics, law enforcement, sports, and the business world. It would be a terrible injustice to many fine people to say that politics and law enforcement in the 1920s were entirely corrupt, but it is perfectly correct to say that there was enough corruption to make the ordinary citizen suspicious of the entire governmental process.

The atmosphere created by this kind of thinking is very much a part of *The Great Gatsby*. The newspapers are an excellent source for understanding the nature of the events that contributed to the disillusionment that underlies the novel. In the following pages we will look at a few major examples.

THE ROSENTHAL MURDER: NICK CARRAWAY
MEETS MEYER WOLFSHEIM

In chapter 4 of *The Great Gatsby*, Meyer Wolfsheim describes the murder of Rosy Rosenthal, which took place in July 1912 and received wide publicity at the time. Fitzgerald's knowledge of the case was almost certainly very thorough because of his friendship with H. Bayard Swope, a reporter for the New York *World* who covered this case as well as many other criminal cases. If it had not been for Swope's persistence, and the publicity he created, the case might never have been solved.

Herman Rosenthal, like many other operators of New York gambling establishments, had been paying protection money to the police. He became an informer and was then shot to death in front of the Metropole Hotel. It was Swope, rather than the suspiciously incompetent police, who took the initiative in solving the case. He was making his usual rounds the night Rosenthal was murdered and hurried to the scene. The chief contribution of the police up to that point had been to arrest the man who had taken down the license number of the getaway car. Swope had already discussed Rosenthal's perilous situation as an informer with Charles Whitman, the district attorney. He now called Whitman and urged him to hurry to the police station. If Whitman had not beaten Lieutenant Charles Becker to the police station, hampering Becker's ability to cover up his own part in the crime, it is quite possible that the case might never have been solved. For it was Becker about whom Rosenthal had been informing, and it was Becker who was eventually executed for Rosenthal's murder, along with the four men who did the actual shooting.

According to Leo Katcher's biography of Rothstein, Rosenthal had at first thought he could topple Becker by testifying to the authorities and taking his story to Swope. Arnold Rothstein, the gambler on whom Meyer Wolfsheim is modeled, was delegated to give Rosenthal $500 and convince him to leave town, but Rosenthal refused. Later, when Rosenthal became frightened, he asked Rothstein for the $500, but Rothstein then refused. It was too late. On the night Becker was put to death, Rothstein and other New

York gamblers stayed up until the sentence was executed, and then went out for their usual night's gambling.

Two newspaper accounts of Rosenthal's murder follow. The New York *Herald Tribune* article describes the murder and gives a brief history of the events leading up to it. As you read it, decide whether or not you think it is intended to be an accusation of Becker or of anyone else. While the *Herald Tribune* article treats the murder as part of a "gambler's war," the coverage in the *New York Times* suggests Becker's guilt much more strongly.

FROM "ROSENTHAL SHOT AND KILLED IN GAMBLER'S WAR"
(New York *Herald Tribune*, July 16, 1912)

Herman Rosenthal, the self-confessed gambler, who was responsible for District Attorney Whitman and Commissioner Waldo to shorten their vacation [*sic*] in order to investigate the graft gambling charges, was shot and instantly killed at 1:55 this morning in front of the Metropole Hotel, in West 43d street, off Broadway. Five bullets were sent through his head, any one of which, according to Dr. Taylor, who responded to an ambulance call from Flower Hospital, would have proven fatal.

"Beansy" Rosenthal, as he was better known to the gambling fraternity, arrived at the hotel and remained there for several hours. At 1:50 o'clock a man came into the hotel, apparently known to the dead man, and asked him to step outside, as a few friends of his wished to see him in regard to some important matter.

In the hotel at the time was Patrolman File, attached to the East 67th street police station, in plain clothes. File said that Rosenthal seemed to hesitate, but later went out rather reluctantly. Just as Rosenthal reached the sidewalk, four shots came in rapid succession.

Fearing that something had gone wrong, File immediately ran out. As he reached the street he met Lieutenant Frye, attached to the West 47th street police station, who was making his rounds about the precinct. The two saw four men hurriedly enter a slate-colored automobile and then head east toward Fifth avenue.

Jumps into Taxicab

A taxicab which was standing near the hotel was immediately pressed into service and the two started after the automobile. Ignoring all traffic regulations, the chauffeur put on all speed. But by this time the machine containing the four men had a good start and was making at least sixty miles an hour, according to the police lieutenant.

For nearly half a mile File and Frye managed to keep the other machine in sight. As it reached 58th street, however, the car turned west, and as they reached the corner they had lost all sight of it.

For some time the taxicab kept running around the various streets in the immediate vicinity, but despite their efforts they were unable to get any trace of the machine.

The five shots that were fired at Rosenthal attracted a large crowd, and a few minutes after the accident the street about the hotel was filled with hundreds of persons. Reserves from several of the nearby stations were turned out to keep them in order.

So far as could be learned, no one around the hotel got a glimpse of the gambler's assailants. That everything had been well planned was the contention of the police, who say ordinarily that there are at least half a dozen taxicabs near the hotel, but when the shooting took place not one was in the vicinity.

Just what File was doing in the hotel could not be ascertained. According to several persons in the hotel he had spent the best part of the evening there.

Go-Between in High Spirits

According to the story told by File the unknown man who lured Rosenthal to his death appeared very jubilant when he appeared at the hotel. He said that Rosenthal was talking to him (File) when the man came in and, after excusing himself asked him to step outside, saying that he was wanted.

Only a few minutes elapsed, File said, after Rosenthal had reached the street when he heard the shooting. He immediately went outside, and directly across the street from the hotel he observed four men entering a machine. With Lieutenant Frye, who appeared on the scene, he said he gave chase but lost them after nearly a mile's pursuit.

Following the shooting, half a dozen detectives were put on the case. File was able to furnish them with a good description of the man who asked Rosenthal out of the hotel, and the police are inclined to believe that the assailants will soon be behind the bars.

The police learned that the man who did the shooting was undersized and swarthy, apparently an Italian. The men in the car had their faces well protected, their hats being pulled down over their foreheads.

District Attorney Whitman and Police Commissioner Waldo, on arriving in town yesterday, began an investigation of the graft gambling charges that cropped up during their absence last week.

Both men made it plain that they had no intention of beginning any criminal or other official proceedings against Lieutenant Charles Becker, of the "strong arm" squad, or any other policeman on the uncorroborated testimony of a gambler.

Commissioner Waldo has taken the position that the charges are of such nature that it is for the District Attorney to act, if he sees fit, and Mr. Whitman admits there is enough in Herman Rosenthal's affidavits to warrant a personal investigation on his part to determine if there is sufficient evidence to warrant a grand jury probe.

Commissioner Waldo courts a full and searching inquiry into his department, being of the opinion that if there is any grafting going on among the police the community would benefit by its exposure. But Mr. Waldo is not willing to accept Rosenthal's charges as Gospel truth solely upon their merits.

In this vein he wrote a letter to District Attorney Whitman, asking for an investigation of Rosenthal's charges, and he ended by saying that "there could be no gambling in this city if the judges and the several district attorneys' offices co-operated with the Police Department."

Doesn't Mean Whitman Himself

The letter made it plain that Mr. Whitman himself was not on Mr. Waldo's blacklist, but when reporters asked Commissioner Waldo for an explanation of the references to judges and district attorneys' offices he refused to go into details, contenting himself by referring his visitors to his letter.

Commissioner Waldo's letter to the District Attorney read:

> I have the honor to request that you cause to be made a thorough investigation of the charges made by a gambler, in the public press, that there has been collusion between certain members of the Police Department and gamblers.
>
> Under the present methods of the department, in order that a gambler might procure protection, it would require the conniving of the inspector of the district and at least three lieutenants in charge of the special squads, all acting independently of each other.
>
> It might be said without fear of contradiction, by fair-minded persons, who have knowledge of the situation, that the city has never been more free from gambling than during the past year. With reference to the public charges made by a self-confessed gambler, that a police lieutenant was in partnership with him, it appears that the lieutenant did his duty in this particular instance, in spite of any alleged entanglements, and that the gambling, the Police Department will afford you every assistance in enforcing the laws [*sic*].

There could be no gambling in the city if the judges and the several District Attorney's officers co-operated with the Police Department as fully as you have personally.

Almost as soon as this letter reached Mr. Whitman, Rosenthal called on the District Attorney and was closeted with him for a little more than a quarter of an hour.

Rosenthal Names Witnesses

Rosenthal said he had given the names of two men to the District Attorney who would be able, he said, to corroborate the charge he made concerning Becker's alleged partnership with him. These two men are said to be Robert H. Hibbard, a lawyer and former policeman, and J. Donahue.

It was in Hibbard's office, in the St. Paul Building, according to Rosenthal, that he signed a mortgage on the furnishing of his gambling house at No. 104 West 45th street in return for a loan of $1,500 which he said Lieutenant Becker made him, and for which Becker insisted that he be made partner in Rosenthal's gambling house, with a 20 per cent interest. Donahue, according to Rosenthal, is the dummy used by Becker to cover him in the transaction.

District Attorney Whitman issued two subpoenas last night, presumably for Hibbard and Donahue, calling for their appearance before him tomorrow.

Lieutenant Becker, after a conference with Commissioner Waldo, received permission to issue a statement in answer to Rosenthal's charges.

"Rosenthal's charges are all mere inventions," said Lieutenant Becker to newspaper men at the office of his counsel, John W. Hart, a former Assistant District Attorney, last night. "I never had any business or social relations with Rosenthal. I met him at the Elks' ball on New Year's eve, and several of his friends practically spoiled my evening by telling me what a good fellow Rosenthal was. Several times after that he extended invitations to me to have dinner with him, but each time I declined. I knew the sort of man he was. I know nothing of the mortgage he speaks of, and Mr. Hibbard never was my lawyer."

Becker's Formal Denial

The statement issued on behalf of Lieutenant Becker by his counsel, Mr. Hart, consisting largely of an attack upon Rosenthal, reads:

It seems unnecessary to dignify the charges of a man like Rosenthal further than to deny the charges absolutely and emphatically, as has already been done. Rosenthal, on his own confession, is a professional criminal, whose whole career, covering a period of many years, in this city has been one of violation of the law. His places have been raided from time to time during the last ten years by the police and he has been prosecuted under different administrations. Each arrest and prosecution has been followed by accusations by Rosenthal similar to the ones made by him against Lieutenant Becker.

In February 1909, when the Police Department attempted to inspect one of his places he complained that he was being "hounded by the police." The District Attorney then had to take Rosenthal in hand and compelled him to admit not only the police but also representatives of the District Attorney's office to his premises. The District Attorney assigned a process server named Emil Klinge to Rosenthal's place, whereupon Rosenthal immediately attempted to bribe Klinge. Upon this being reported to Mr. Jerome he directed Klinge to accept the money offered, which Klinge did, and this transaction resulted in the indictment of Rosenthal for bribery. Klinge, I believe, is still employed by the District Attorney.

When Rosenthal's place was raided last November by Inspector Hayes and Captain Day he again charged that he was "framed up," and procured summonses from Chief Magistrate McAdoo against the two officers, but later withdrew his charge.

I am informed that in 1909 Rosenthal was excluded by the stewards of the Jockey Club from the Empire City racetrack because he had refused to pay a bet that had been made with him.

I believe this offence is technically known as "welching." The accusations made by Rosenthal against former Deputy Commissioner Driscoll's two police officers are recent enough to be remembered. These facts, taken in connection with the two pending cases against Rosenthal's gambling resorts, together with his confession that he is in that business, would seem to furnish the only answer required to his accusations.

A statement that a police officer had a 20 per cent interest in Rosenthal's gambling house and that he raided and closed that gambling house on the 15th of April, that it had been kept closed by the police ever since, and that the lieutenant of police who closed it and had that 20 percent interest in the business paid $1,500 for the privilege of closing it, is so preposterous upon its face that it seems to require no answer whatsoever. Further facts concerning Rosenthal's career are being investigated and may be given out later.

My client courts the fullest investigation of these charges, although it would be a great injustice to require him to defend himself from such transparently malicious accusations. Should any responsible public officer see fit to act upon them, Lieutenant Becker will meet them fully and squarely, and will show, moreover, that they are due to his efficient performance of his duties.

Donahue Mortgage Found

District Attorney Whitman refused to say last night if Hibbard would be called as a witness. He admitted, however, that a record of the Donahue mortgage had been found. Hibbard was out of town yesterday and is not expected back until to-day.

Just before leaving his office for the day Mr. Whitman made it clear that he would not institute any grand jury proceeding on Rosenthal's word.

"I have no intention of wasting the grand jury's time," said Mr. Whitman, "by presenting to them the testimony of witnesses whose statements consist of little more than rumor or hearsay, but this office stands ready to proceed on any proper evidence, properly corroborated, which involves the corruption of the Police Department or any other city department."

Rosenthal again appeared before Magistrate Butts, in the West Side court, yesterday, and presented an additional affidavit charging police oppression and asking for warrants for the arrest of Inspector Hayes and Captain Day for maintaining a uniformed policeman day and night at his former gambling house since the night of the last raid. The court reserved decision.

Rosenthal told the newspaper men yesterday that messengers from politicians and policemen had been visiting him frequently the last forty-eight hours urging him to leave town.

"They told me I had gone far enough and to beat it," said Rosenthal. "But I'm going to stick. This is a fight to the finish."

His counsel, Joseph S. Rosenback, submitted to Magistrate Butts an opinion written by Mayor Gaynor when he was on the Supreme Court bench deciding that the police had no right to keep a policeman in a man's home or place of business.

FROM "GAMBLER WHO DEFIED POLICE IS SHOT DEAD"
(*New York Times*, July 16, 1912)

• • •

In the great throng which rushed from all parts of Times Square at the sound of the shots and who gathered around the fallen man were many who recognized him, and like a flash the news sped through the crowd:

"It is Herman Rosenthal, the gambler who defied Lieut. Becker of the police Strong Arm Squad."

It was Rosenthal, the man who on Thursday night locked a policeman in his home at 104 West Forty-fifth street, declaring that he had determined to bring to an end the police guard on his premises, which was instituted last April 15, when Becker and his squad raided the house as a gambling place. It was Rosenthal who since Friday had carried his case to the courts, and as recently as yesterday afternoon had been in consultation with District Attorney Whitman, to whom he offered to produce proof of his allegations that Lieut. Becker had been a silent partner in his place. It was Rosenthal who declared yesterday that the whole police world was on edge because of the "disclosures," and that he had no sleep the night before, so many were the messages urging him to get out of town. It was Rosenthal who admitted yesterday that the whole gambling fraternity was bitter against him, his attitude being interpreted by them as the wail of an embittered and thwarted climber from downtown disappointed at his failure to break into the uptown gambling section. It was Rosenthal, more famous yesterday than ever in his career, who lay dead on the sidewalk.

• • •

Policeman "Baker" Warned Him

Persons in the Rosenthal home declared after the shooting that Rosenthal had been warned to leave town if he cared for his life. They also said that Mrs. Rosenthal, when she heard of the shooting, declared that only yesterday afternoon a "Policeman Baker" had warned her husband that he would be killed if he did not leave town.

THE MURDER OF ARNOLD ROTHSTEIN

Rothstein was still a fairly small operator at the time of Rosenthal's murder, but in the next few years he became the chief financier of crime in New York City. He was involved in gambling, bootlegging, labor racketeering, and crooked stock deals, among other things. Though he was often implicated and subpoenaed, his guilt remained unproved. One of his major involvements was with E. M. Fuller and Company, which went bankrupt with no assets. Investors lost $5 million. Although Rothstein was forced to appear before a grand jury and was even indicted for perjury and income tax evasion, he was never tried. The brief hints about bond swindles in *The Great Gatsby* probably have their origin in this case.

Rothstein, like Rosenthal, was eventually murdered. He was shot on November 4, 1928, and died two days later without saying who had killed him. His murder remains unsolved. George McManus, to whose hotel room Rothstein went on the night he was killed, was tried for the crime. The judge gave a directed verdict of innocent because he believed that there was not even enough evidence for the jury to consider. Rothstein probably was murdered because he had stalled on paying a gambling debt. On September 9, two months before he was killed, he had lost well over $200,000 in a poker game. Although he dealt in much larger sums than this, he was often short of ready cash. He may have believed the game was crooked, and he may have thought that by stalling he could pick up his IOU's at a discount. Then, too, he felt that anyone as important as himself should pay when he felt like it. But this theory raises some difficulties. For one thing, as Nate Raymond, one of the creditors, said, to kill Rothstein was to lose all hope of collecting the money.

Rothstein's murder had staggering repercussions. Between his death in November 1928 and the acquittal of his alleged killer on December 6, 1929, approximately two hundred articles about the case appeared in the *New York Times* alone. (The following account of the crime and investigation relies heavily on Donald Clarke's *In the Reign of Rothstein* and Leo Katcher's *The Big Bankroll*.) The 40,000 papers Rothstein left behind showed connections to bond theft, insurance fraud, narcotics traffic, and varieties of gambling as well as many other things. Among those who owed him money were gangsters, lawyers, clothing manufacturers, theater and restaurant owners, and private detectives. His papers pointed to many supposedly respectable citizens.

On the night of November 4, Rothstein had dinner with his girlfriend, Inez Norton. (He was separated from his wife, who was planning to divorce him.) Norton then went to a movie, and Rothstein went to Lindy's restaurant and club. He received a phone call at about 10:30 P.M. asking him to go to the hotel room of George McManus. The September game in which he had lost had been played in McManus' hotel room. Before going to the hotel room he left his pistol with a friend. At about 10:50 P.M. Rothstein was found leaning against a wall in the hotel room, saying that he had been shot and asking for an ambulance. He died about 10:20 A.M. on November 6. Although he was at times conscious, he would not name his killer.

The case had puzzling contradictions. McManus immediately went into hiding for three weeks with the Dutch Schultz gang and then turned himself in. This would seem to indicate gang involvement. But gangsters usually fill their victims with bullets. Rothstein was shot only once. Katcher relates a story common among gamblers—that Rothstein had been confronted by someone drunk and hysterical who had a gun. The gun had gone off when Rothstein had tried to take it away. But the bullet had entered Rothstein's body from behind. This makes the gambler's theory unlikely, but not entirely beyond the realm of possibility.

According to the gamblers' code, McManus, as host for the game, was responsible for making Rothstein pay. Twice McManus had sent men to collect, and twice Rothstein had brushed them off. McManus claimed not to have been in the room when Rothstein was shot. The gamblers to whom Rothstein owed money all had alibis. One witness, a hotel maid named Bridget Farry, placed McManus in the room with Rothstein. She was held as a material witness without bail until the trial. By then she would no longer identify McManus.

A further complication occurred when Fats Walsh, who had once been Rothstein's bodyguard, was murdered. Although he no longer worked for Rothstein, he was at Lindy's the night of November 4, and it was he who called Mrs. Rothstein to tell her that

her husband had been shot. The police saw no connection between the murder of Rothstein and that of his bodyguard. Mc-
Manus remains the most likely suspect. But to kill Rothstein was
to lose the money. Why did the Dutch Schultz gang hide McManus
for three weeks? Why did he then turn himself in?

Leo Katcher believes that gang control had become so strong in
New York and that Rothstein's affairs had become so involved that
those in power did not want a real investigation. Mayor Jimmie
Walker noisily insisted that the case was not being handled properly and fired Police Commissioner Joseph Warren. Warren's reluctant replacement, Grover Whalen, produced no new evidence
and blamed the failure to solve the case on poor police work at
the time of the murder. Because Bridget Farry, the only important
witness against McManus, had changed her testimony, there was
no way to place McManus in the room with Rothstein.

The following coverage from the *New York Times* gives an idea
of how the trial of McManus went. Notice that Bridget Farry, who
had originally identified McManus as the man in the room with
Rothstein, has changed her story entirely. She is now hostile toward the prosecution and even accuses the prosecutors of trying
to bribe her. (They had given her ten dollars for cab fare.) She is
now very friendly toward McManus. Perhaps her change of attitude
was the result of anger. She had been locked up for a year because
she was a material witness, and no one would put up bail for her.
If anything else had happened to change her mind—a bribe or a
threat or both, perhaps—nothing was ever proven.

FROM "COURT TO HEAR PLEA TO VOID INDICTMENT OF
M'MANUS TODAY"
(*New York Times*, December 5, 1929)

A motion to dismiss the indictment charging George A. McManus with
the murder of Arnold Rothstein will be made today by James D. C. Murray, attorney for the defense. The plea will be made on the ground that
the State has failed to make out a case against the accused man.

Announcement of his intention was made by Mr. Murray yesterday afternoon after Assistant District Attorney George N. Brothers had said the
State would rest its case today and the trial judge, Charles C. Nott Jr.,
had suggested a flaw in the prosecution's chain of circumstantial evi-

dence. Mr. Brothers declared that all of the evidence against the defendant had been introduced except the testimony of a small-arms expert on the alleged murder weapon.

Bringing his case to the last chapter, Mr. Brothers had called Mrs. Bridget Farry and James Meehan to the stand. The former chambermaid of the Park Central Hotel, where the State says Rothstein received his death wound, denied that McManus had been the "Mac" she had seen in the room where the State charges the shooting took place. Meehan testified that Rothstein went to the hotel with a revolver exactly like the alleged murder weapon.

Arms Expert to Testify

The prosecution will offer the expert testimony on the revolver this morning, although Judge Nott, in adjourning the trial yesterday, made it quite clear that he felt the District Attorney had failed utterly to connect the revolver with McManus. Nevertheless, said District Attorney Banton, the proof would be offered and the effort to have the indictment thrown out would be fought.

It was when Mrs. Farry, gathering the folds of a vivid green gown about her, stepped down from the stand as the last witness of the day, that Mr. Brothers and Assistant District Attorney James McDonald moved to the bench of Judge Nott and conferred. They talked to the court for fifteen minutes and then resumed their seats at the prosecution table.

• • •

[As the judge had indicated, it proved impossible to link McManus with the pistol in question. The only real evidence now remaining was the testimony of Bridget Farry.]

Mrs. Farry took the stand with a flounce, as if eager to take reprisal for the months she spent in jail in default of $10,000 bail as a material witness. She did not wear the gold crown she had said she would don for the occasion, but her bearing was regal.

The quondam chambermaid was an eye-filling vision of emerald green. She wore a georgette gown of Erin hue and a large green bow in her tousled black hair, a coy curl of which graced her left shoulder. Bridget spoke with a brogue and her anger made it strident. Her black eyes snapped with indignation—until the soft-voiced Mr. Murray took her in hand.

Then, no longer facing her arch-enemies, Mr. Brothers and Mr. McDonald ("and with a name like that," as she once said), Mrs. Farry's belligerency receded. She swore with emphatic assurance that McManus had not been the man named "Mac," and looked admiringly at the de-

fendant—a fine broth of a boy—as he turned slowly around for her negative identification.

Glares at Prosecutor

The witness, dark, plump and youthful of face, had a grim look about her as she sat down on the extreme edge of the witness chair and turned a glare loose at Mr. Brothers. The prosecutor favored Mrs. Farry with a sugary smile, but she would have none of his peace overtures.

"Mrs. Farry," he cooed, "were you employed in the Park Central Hotel?"

"Yes," said Mrs. Farry in a tone not remotely resembling cooing.

"For how long, Mrs. Farry?"

"Four months."

"In November, 1928?"

"Yes, I was."

"What was the nature of your work?"

"Chambermaid."

"What were your duties?"

"Chambermaid's work," said Mrs. Farry, looking as if anybody would know that.

"Do you recall Sunday night, Nov. 4, 1928?"

"Yes."

"What time did you go to work?"

"Nine o'clock in the morning."

"And you worked until when?"

"Midnight."

"On what floor did you work, Mrs. Farry?"

"On the third floor on the day shift, which was until 4 o'clock in the day and then that and other rooms until midnight."

Mr. Brothers asked if she remembered Room 349. She did, said the witness, and she had occasion to go into it several times that day and evening. When was the first time? asked the Assistant District Attorney.

"Well, the first time," said the witness, "was around 9 o'clock in the morning. I noticed that a table was by the door and I moved it into the hall. I noticed that the door was ajar maybe three or four inches. I could hear some one asleep inside. That was at 9 o'clock in the morning."

"Did you see anyone?"

"No."

"When did you go back?"

"I don't remember the time, but I went back and I put the key in the door. A man came to the door and I said 'Do you want your bed made?' and he said that he didn't care. I went in and made up the one bed that had been slept in. There was a coat on a chair, over the back."

Man Said He Was "Mac"

"The man spoke to me about Ireland and he said his name was 'Mac.'
I turned my back on him and went on with my work."

"Did you return to the room later?"

"I went back when I got a 'checkout' from downstairs."

"What time was that?"

"It was 8 o'clock at night."

"How many times in all during that day did you go in Room 349?"

"Three or four times."

"Now this man 'Mac,' was he in there on all the occasions when you
entered that room—was it the same man?"

"There were two men in there on one time."

"Was it the same man?"

"I don't know; I didn't take any notice of him."

"Did you see the same man during that day?"

This insistence by Mr. Brothers on "the same man" riled Mrs. Farry
considerably. A flush crept across her pale, broad face and she registered
other "danger signals" which Mr. Brothers apparently was quick to de-
tect. He recalled that Mrs. Farry, in describing the man she had seen in
the morning on her second call at the room, had said that he had been
shaving.

"Was he dressed?" said Mr. Brothers.

"Well, he had on a shirt and a pair of pants," said Mrs. Farry, bridling.

Saw Two Men in Room 349

"Now, at 8 P.M., who was there?"

"Two men."

"What were they like?"

"One was a short man and the other was a tall man."

"Was the man shaving in the morning a short man?"

"He was."

"Was the tall man in the morning who talked to you about Ireland the
same tall man you saw at night?"

"Yes."

"He is the man who said his name was 'Mac'?"

"Yes."

"What was the first time you spoke to the occupant of Room 349 about
a check-out?"

"It was at 8 o'clock. He said, 'Not yet—in a short time.' "

"What were the two men doing?"

"They were talking."

"Were they sitting down or standing?"

"I think they were sitting down."

"Did you hear either of them telephoning?"

"Well, the telephone rang and I thought it was the linen room. I had the check-out slip and thought they wanted me. I answered the telephone and I said to the big man, 'I think this is for you, sir.' "

Mrs. Farry later disclosed that the call had been from a woman.

"Did either of the men telephone for anything to drink?"

"Not while I was there."

"When was the next time you visited the room?"

"It was twenty minutes past 10 o'clock that night. The big man asked what time it was, and I telephoned down and said a guest wants to know what time it is."

"How many men were in the room then?"

"Two men."

Unable to Identify McManus

"You can see this defendant, George McManus, can't you? Was he one of the men?"

"Will you have him stand up?"

Mrs. Farry edged halfway off her chair to get a good, thorough look at McManus. The defendant, smiling broadly, stood up. Bridget gazed at him for a minute or so.

"That's not the man," she said with conviction.

"Are you sure of that?"

"I am."

"Are you willing to swear on your oath that this defendant is not the man?"

"I am—he's not the man."

"Do you know that this defendant admitted yesterday that he was the occupant of—"

Mr. Murray registered an objection and was sustained by Judge Nott.

"Did you see [t]his defendant in the City Prison?" continued the prosecutor.

"I didn't identify him," said Mrs. Farry quickly.

"Now Mrs. Farry, didn't you identify this defendant in the City Prison—in the Tombs over there?"

"I didn't identify anybody."

"Did you place your hand on this man in the line-up over there?"

"They carried me to the line-up and I put my hand on a man, but that's all."

"They carried you—how much do you weigh, Mrs. Farry?"

Mrs. Farry let that one go by with composure and with contempt muttering merely, "Never mind what I weigh."

"Didn't you identify this man?" persisted Mr. Brothers.

The reiteration was too much for the witness. She gave her head a shake which added to the confusion of her hair.

Witness Accuses Detectives

"They wanted me to frame somebody and I wouldn't do it," she said.

"Who wanted you to frame somebody?"

"The detectives."

Mr. Brothers reverted to the 10:20 visit of the witness to Room 349. The witness said that five minutes after she reached the room, the "big man" walked out.

"He gave me 75 cents," she testified, "and asked me to go down and have dinner with him because I had been working all day."

"Where were you?"

"I was in the hallway. I had walked down the hallway and there were two young fellows standing at the elevators and one of them said to me, 'Have some schnapps?' and I said to him, 'What do you mean—who are you?' And I went on down the hall and the big man was walking along it, too."

"He was going out?"

"He was."

"How about the other man in the room?"

"I don't know about him."

The Assistant District Attorney sought to shake Mrs. Farry on this episode, but she clung to her testimony. Mr. Brothers began to show signs of impatience.

"Madame," he said, dropping his urbanity, "did you come here to tell the truth?"

"I did."

"Let me ask you this—you are very angry at the police in this case because you were locked up as a material witness, aren't you?"

Charges Attempt to Bribe Her

Mrs. Farry saw her chance. She grasped her handbag tightly and leaned forward. Her snapping eyes bore into Mr. Brothers.

"I am," she said with steadily rising inflection. "I am angry at you, too, and all the rest of them. I would not do what you wanted me to do."

"You are angry with me?" said Mr. Brothers incredulously.

"Yes, I am, and after you tried to bribe me"—

"I tried to bribe you?" said the amazed prosecutor.

"Yes, and you can have your $10 back."

Mrs. Farry pulled up her handbag and took a look at its contents.

"Tell the jury all about it," counseled Mr. Brothers.

"I will," said the witness, drawing her lips to a faint line.

The witness finally found what she sought. It was a $10 note neatly folded. She tossed it to the stenographer's desk in front of her with withering scorn.

"There's your dirty money," she said.

Mr. Brothers picked it up. He unfolded it and studied it.

"This is Mr. McDonald's $10, isn't it?" he asked.

"Yes, it is."

"Do you mind," Mr. Brothers inquired politely, "if I give it back to Mr. McDonald?"

"No, go ahead. That's why I gave it to you."

As Mr. McDonald bowed and pocketed the money court attendants went about busily trying to still the laughter.

It developed later that the money had been given to Mrs. Farry to defray her taxicab fare—she no longer patronizes any other form of transportation—after she had complained of the cost of riding to court from her home in La Fontaine Avenue, the Bronx.

"You couldn't buy my oath for $10—no, not for a million dollars," said Mrs. Farry, as, assuming a more comfortable posture, [she] displayed pink stockings and gold slippers.

The examiner then tried to show, by reading from her testimony before the grand jury, that the witness had told a different story of the events at the Park Central on the night of the shooting of Rothstein. He did not get very far, the witness, with her capable hands folded in her lap, stoutly insisting that she was telling the truth.

FROM "M'MANUS ACQUITTED BY ORDER OF COURT OF
KILLING ROTHSTEIN"
(*New York Times*, December 6, 1929)

*Nott, Granting Defense Motion, Says State Had Failed to
Establish Case
Prosecutor Admits It
He and Court Declare Most of State Witnesses Were Hostile and
Untruthful*

Judge Charles C. Nott Jr. directed the jury in General Sessions Court at 10:47 A.M. yesterday to acquit George A. McManus of the murder of Arnold Rothstein. The State had failed to establish its case against the defendant, said the judge, and there was no alternative except to free him. Thus the killing of the gambler was obscured again in the mists of unsolved crime.

Standing erect before the twelve men in the jury box, McManus heard the foreman, Herman Sherman, formally render the verdict which cleared him a year and three days after he had been indicted. The defendant's face flushed and he tried to smile. He failed and tears came into his eyes.

As the jurors filed rapidly out of the court McManus turned. He waved to his brothers, blew a kiss to his wife and asked that the news be rushed to his elderly mother in the Bronx. "Tell mama right away," he whispered to one of his brothers, Stephen.

"Naturally I am happy," he said to reporters.

"We produced everything we had," said District Attorney Banton, somewhat sadly.

"It only shows that you can't prove something that didn't exist," was the comment of the defense attorney, James Murray.

Jurors Would Have Freed Him

"We would have found him not guilty on the evidence anyway," chorused the jurors.

"I was sure of it—nothing else but," said Mrs. George McManus, clinging to her husband's hand and crying and laughing by turns.

While the verdict means that McManus can never be tried again, said Assistant District Attorney George N. Brothers, the murder of Rothstein will not be dropped.

• • •

The complete collapse of the prosecution, an admission of failure by Mr. Brothers, who blamed the hostility of witnesses and the rendering of the verdict which set McManus free, took just fifteen minutes. The defendant in his limousine was en route to his mother's home ten minutes later. Within a half-hour the court room held only attendants noisily putting chairs back in place—and the trial, to determine who shot Rothstein on the night of Nov. 4, 1928, in Room 349 of the Park Central Hotel, had passed into the limbo of legal history.

THE 1919 WORLD SERIES SCANDAL

The World Series scandal was heartbreaking to the sports-minded American public. It is mentioned directly in *The Great Gatsby* when Gatsby tells Nick Carraway in chapter 4 that Meyer Wolfsheim is the man who fixed the World Series. The 1919 World Series actually *had* been fixed, probably by large-scale gambler Arnold Rothstein, who served as a model for Wolfsheim. Rothstein was publicly accused by American League president Ban Johnson of fixing the series. Rothstein appeared before the grand jury that indicted eight White Sox players and claimed he had been offered a chance to invest $100,000 to pay for the fix but had refused the offer. He was not indicted. At this point the accounts become contradictory. Rothstein's biographer, Leo Katcher, believes Rothstein was telling the truth, but according to Donald Gropman, the biographer of accused ballplayer Joe Jackson, an examination of Rothstein's papers after his murder revealed that he spent $80,000 arranging the fix. This was only one of several occasions when Rothstein appeared before grand juries. In most cases he avoided indictment. Guilty or not, he was fixed in the minds of the American public as the man who had corrupted its most loved sport at the highest level.

Fitzgerald skillfully gives the impression that Wolfsheim is a major figure in organized crime, as was Rothstein. Fitzgerald, who had met Rothstein, deliberately made Wolfsheim cruder and less attractive than his model. To someone of Fitzgerald's elite Princeton background, Rothstein may have seemed crude, but others have described him as graceful and as tastefully dressed.

It is hard for a reader today to comprehend what a blow this scandal was. Baseball was then the almost universally followed American sport. It would be years before football overshadowed it. The public, and especially children, idolized baseball players.

Eight Chicago White Sox players were indicted for taking bribes to lose the 1919 World Series to the Cincinnati Reds. Although most of them were probably guilty, all were finally acquitted. Nonetheless, the commissioner of baseball, Judge Kennesaw Mountain Landis, removed them from major league baseball before the trial, and they were never reinstated. Shoeless Joe Jackson, the most famous, admired, and colorful of the eight, was supposedly confronted by a small boy begging, "Say it ain't so, Joe!" Joe could not say it was not so.

Actually, there is considerable evidence that the illiterate Jackson was guilty of ignorance and bumbling rather than of complete dishonesty. Jackson first heard of a fix and asked White Sox owner Charles Albert Comiskey to keep him out of the series, but Comiskey told him to play and ignore the rumors. Nothing in Jackson's performance suggested that he threw the games. Another player who had approached him earlier gave him $5,000 after the series. To help disguise his client's previous knowledge, Alfred Austrian, Comiskey's lawyer, convinced Jackson that his only hope was to confess and beg for mercy. The testimony Jackson then gave the grand jury was muddled, and part of the grand jury records mysteriously disappeared before the trial. The players took the Fifth Amendment (refusing to testify on the grounds that their answers might incriminate them), and Abe Attell, accused as an organizer and a go-between in arranging the bribery, went to Canada and refused to return to testify. Attell had once worked as Rothstein's bodyguard.

The following articles from the Chicago *Tribune* show how the various accusations and counteraccusations led to the grand jury investigations. The investigations may have been futile in the sense that no one was convicted, but the lives of the accused players were ruined, and the reputation of the nation's favorite sport was smeared.

FROM JAMES CRUSINBERRY, "FIVE WHITE SOX MEN INVOLVED,
HOYNE AID SAYS"
(Chicago *Tribune*, September 23, 1920)

Revelations Made by Player Herzog

Charles L. Herzog, infielder of the Cubs, last night unfolded a story, supported by copies of sworn depositions and a letter that may go far toward clearing up the reports of alleged crookedness in baseball not only in games in which the Cubs were concerned, but in the world's series of last fall between the White Sox and the Cincinnati Reds.

Herzog, accompanied by Fred Merkle, Claude Hendrix, and Nick Carter, arrived in Chicago yesterday afternoon, having been sent home direct from Boston while the team went to New York to finish the eastern tour.

A peculiar coincidence is the fact that the depositions disclose as damaging evidence against the world's series of last fall as has yet come to light. Two National league players in sworn statements say they heard another admit having been "tipped" off that Cincinnati would win the first two games and the series.

Grand Jury Starts Grinding

In the baseball investigation opened by the Cook county grand jury the name of Herzog was whispered about the ante-room as being connected in some way with the scandals. The rumor was that he had offered Rube Benton, pitcher of the Giants, $800 last September to "throw" a game to the Cubs. Gamblers throughout the country bet heavily on the New York club. If the Cubs could win the bookmakers would collect a large amount. The story was that a pool was made up and an emissary sent to Benton. The "bribe offer" was indignantly refused, according to reports, and for protection Benton made a memorandum of the matter and reported it to the officials of his club.

Benton has been summoned to appear before the grand jury and is expected to arrive from New York this morning and report at the Criminal Court building at 11 o'clock.

Benton probably will be questioned regarding his alleged statement that Herzog attempted to bribe him, and also regarding the affidavits in Herzog's possession, which assert Benton won $3,800 by betting on Cincinnati during the world's series after a tip he received from Hal Chase.

The first day's work of the grand jury included the hearing of testimony from Ban Johnson, president of the American league, and Charles A. Comiskey and William L. Veeck, presidents of the two Chicago teams. Several baseball reporters also were heard.

Though it had been understood the inquiry would be public the usual grand jury secrecy was observed and just what the witnesses told was not given out.

However, it is known that important evidence was uncovered. Assistant State's Attorney Hartley L. Replogle, in charge of the inquiry, declared that "some very good stuff" was brought out, and that the grand jurors were successful in obtaining information tending to throw light on charges that certain players had accepted money from gamblers and played in such a manner as to lose ball games.

"The last world's series between the Chicago White Sox and the Cincinnati Reds was not on the square," said Replogle. "From five to seven players on the White Sox team are involved."

Herzog, seated in a café in company with Merkle, last night detailed the story of the alleged attempt to "fix" a Cub game and produced the depositions of Art Wilson and Norman "Toney" Boeckel, members of the

Boston Braves, who as friends of Herzog made sworn statements regarding a conversation they had with Rube Benton in New York early this season, Benton being the accuser of Herzog.

In the depositions, made in Chicago on May 17, it is disclosed that Benton, being "tipped off" last fall by Hal Chase that the Reds would beat the White Sox in the world's series, had scraped up as much money as he could, had wagered on Cincinnati, and had won some $3,800.

Herzog declared he obtained the affidavits from his friends because Benton last spring had declared to John McGraw, manager of the Giants, that he never had been connected with betting on baseball, McGraw demanding such a promise before agreeing to take him back as a member of the team.

Herzog also produced a letter from President Heydler of the National league in which the latter stated he had been convinced that Herzog did not have any connection with gambling on baseball. This letter was dated June 25, after Heydler, according to Herzog's story, had thrashed the matter out with both Benton and Herzog in his office, finally declaring the whole thing should be dropped and kept quiet.

Here Is Herzog's Story

Herzog's story, as told by himself, follows:

"Last May, when the Boston club was in Chicago, Art Wilson stopped me after one of the games and said he wanted to talk to me. I suggested we have dinner together and after we were at the table in a downtown restaurant, Art said:

"Buck, there is something I want to talk to you about and I don't know just how to say it."

"I assured him if he needed some money I would be glad to help him, but he waved the idea of money away and told me he had heard rumors among the ball players in the east that Benton had said I offered him $800 last September to throw a game to the Cubs. That was the first I had heard of it. He related some of the details of Benton's story and I immediately asked Wilson if he would go with me the next day to President Veeck of the Cubs and relate the same story.

Calls for Showdown

"Art agreed and the next day we went to Veeck's office. I asked Wilson to tell Veeck just what he had told me and Wilson did. Then Veeck replied he had heard of the affair a couple of weeks before. I told Veeck I thought he should have talked to me about it at once and I asked him to have President Heydler come on from New York when the Giants would be in Chicago a few days later; that I would demand a hearing before Heydler in the presence of Benton. Before the Boston club left I got Wilson and Boeckel to make the depositions regarding Benton so I might show them to Heydler.

"Veeck agreed to ask Heydler to come, but after some days of delay, informed me Heydler couldn't, but would take the thing up when we got to New York in June.

"The first day we were in New York I went to Heydler's office. He promised to get Benton there the next day. The next day Benton wasn't there, but the following day he was.

Bares Benton's Affidavit

"He had already filed an affidavit with Heydler declaring that he, Hal Chase and myself during the previous September, when the Giants were playing in Chicago, had gone in a taxi to a saloon, and that there in a back room in the presence of Chase and the short stout proprietor of the saloon, I had offered him $800 to throw the game the next day to the Cubs.

"I found out afterward that Benton couldn't tell where the saloon was, but he said it was Stillson's.

"I demanded from Heydler the right to cross question Benton and asked him if he remembered having pried open my desk in Cincinnati when I was manager of the Reds and he was a member of that team, and obtaining the pay roll of the Cincinnati club, then joking the players in the clubhouse by telling most of them the exact amount of their salaries. He remembered it and admitted the act.

Charges Threat by "Rube"

"I asked him if he remembered being in a poker game on the train when with the Cincinnati club, and getting into an argument with Doc Miller; of pulling a knife and starting to attack Miller; then, after being considerably damaged in the fight, of having Miller dress his bruises and how, when I fined both him and Miller $50 for their actions, he declared he 'would get me some day for that.' He remembered.

"I asked him if he remembered having said, previous to a game at Cubs park in last September's series between the Cubs and Giants, 'Boys, watch me win today.' He remembered that, and that was the series in which I was supposed to have offered him the $800.

"Then I told him in front of Heydler why he said that. It wasn't because of any bribe; it was because he had been caught breaking the rules of the club on the previous night by Manager McGraw, and McGraw had told him he would pitch the next day; that he had better win or it would go tough with him.

Ready for Finish Fight

"Well, when Heydler heard all this he turned on Benton, gave him a calling, and said the whole matter should be dropped and kept quiet. I thought that indicated he didn't believe Benton's yarn, and Mr. Heydler followed by giving me a letter in which he said he wouldn't find that I had been connected with gambling in any way.

"That happened in June. I would have been willing to give the whole story to the press then. Now it has come back and made things look as though I were connected with crookedness in baseball.

"I propose to see the thing through to the finish."

Hal Chase was dropped by the Giants last spring with Heine Zimmerman, but Manager McGraw never stated why. Since then Chase has been barred from the parks of the Coast league because of alleged dealings with gamblers and ball players.

The Grand Jury Hearing

Before he went before the grand jury yesterday afternoon Ban Johnson admitted he had evidence that there had been crooked ball games last year and that several players had been expelled from the big leagues as a result. He had no direct evidence of any "thrown" games this year, he said.

What Mr. Comiskey testified to was not learned. The baseball reporters generally agreed in a disbelief that crookedness in baseball players was in any sense general.

John J. (Muggsy) McGraw, manager of the New York Giants, and Barry McCormick, umpire in the Philadelphia-Cub game of Aug. 31, will be requested to testify next week.

"McGraw knows not only about the Lee Magee matter, but about other things," said Prosecutor Replogle. "We also intend to ask Charles Stoneham, president of the Giants, and Joseph Vila of the New York Sun to come voluntarily as witnesses."

Loser on the Sox to Appear

Samuel W. Pass, a manufacturer in the Peoples Gas building, an ardent Sox fan and a close friend of many of the Sox players, is also to be called. That he had lost a large sum on the Sox during the world's series and had since learned some of the things responsible for the losing of the series was brought out in the hearing.

The reports of the detective agency which was employed by the Cub team after the "scandal" broke with regard to the Aug. 31 game, was [sic] turned over to the authorities by Mr. Veeck, president of the club. That he discussed the game before the jury and told how Grover Cleveland

Alexander was sent in to pitch when informed that that game was to be fixed, was admitted. He also was asked concerning the replacing of Merkle by Barber and the playing of Herzog, whose error in the game was costly.

That in all probability no indictments will result from the investigation was admitted by the authorities. If they can purge the game of any taint of scandal they will have accomplished a great deal, they say. Judge McDonald, who ordered the investigation, declared it was solely for the good of the sport.

FROM "PLAN PROBE OF COHAN-TENNES LOSSES ON SOX"
(Chicago *Tribune*, September 24, 1920)

Dropped $110,000 on Series, Report

George M. Cohan, the actor, and Mont Tennes, the Chicago gambler, both of whom were heavy losers in games in the last world's series, which it is charged was "fixed," are expected to be asked by the Cook county grand jury to tell what they know of the efforts of gamblers to corrupt professional baseball.

An inside story that Mr. Cohan informed friends of a loss of $30,000 on games which his own investigations have since indicated were "thrown" will be placed before the grand jury.

Reports fix the amount that Tennes lost on the last world's series at $80,000.

"Series Crooked"—Hoyne

In New York State's Attorney Hoyne said the statement that Cohan and Tennes had information regarding baseball crookedness would be thoroughly investigated by his office and that "if the inquiry warrants it their presence will be sought.

"Judging from a preliminary investigation," Mr. Hoyne added, "I have no doubt the 1919 world's series was crooked and that at least one Chicago player was crooked.

"Judge McDonald, the judicial head of the grand jury's investigation, is 100 per cent square, and the public may be assured everything will be done to get to the bottom of the thing that justice may be done to baseball and gambling be eradicated."

Jury Foreman "Shocked"

Henry H. Brigham, foreman of the grand jury, made a similar statement at the close of the day's investigations.

"Chicago, New York, Cincinnati and St. Louis gamblers are bleeding baseball and corrupting players," he said. "We are going the limit in this inquiry, but at present we cannot give out the evidence we have uncovered. I am shocked at the rottenness so far revealed."

Benton Bares "Bribe Offer"

The star witness at yesterday's grand jury session was Jacob C. "Rube" Benton. The hurler for the New York Giants told in detail of being offered a bribe to lose a game. He named "Buck" Herzog, Hal Chase, and Heine Zimmerman in connection with the offer.

Samuel W. Pass, the manufacturer, who is declared to be closer to the White Sox players than any person aside from Manager Gleason, was before the inquisitors for an hour and a half. Persons in the anteroom surmised the jurors were impressed with his story when vigorous applause was heard from the jury room.

Benton before entering the jury room denied he had won $3,800 on the last world's series on a "tipoff" by Chase, who, according to Herzog's statement Wednesday night, had sent Benton a telegram advising him to wager on the Cincinnati Reds to beat the White Sox.

Johnson Stirs Sensation

Ban Johnson, president of the American league, admitted last night he had "heard statements that the White Sox would not dare to win the 1920 pennant because the managers of a gambling syndicate, alleged to have certain players in their power, had forbidden it."

His remarks caused a sensation, coming at a time when Chicago and Cleveland are locked in a struggle for the pennant. The gamblers are credited with having backed Cleveland heavily. The Sox, by winning yesterday, are within half a game of the lead, and if they go to first place the gamblers will have to stand heavy losses.

Certain Sox players who have heard the report are said to have been spurred on to make every effort to win as a vindication, regardless of athletic honors or monetary reward.

Jury to Recall Johnson

Announcement was made at the state's attorney's office, following adjournment of the grand jury, that Mr. Johnson will be recalled to tell what he knows of a gambling-blackmailing plot against the Sox, if one exists. If the reports can be corroborated, a new and dangerous kind of blackmail will have been exposed, it was declared.

President Johnson in his statement also admitted knowledge of the holding up of the salary checks of eight Sox players following the 1919 world's series. He said three, Chick Gandil, Eddie Cicotte, and Fred McMullin, had asked his assistance in obtaining their money from Charles A. Comiskey, president of the Sox.

Regarding the possibility that gamblers have a grip on a number of Sox players, Mr. Johnson said:

"I heard several weeks ago a vague statement that the White Sox would not dare win the pennant this season. That statement was repeated several times, and within the last few weeks it has been hinted, more or less openly, that the Sox would not dare win because the gambling syndicate would tell what it knew of certain players in the Cincinnati-Sox world's championship games in 1919."

In order to vindicate themselves with Chicago fans, various baseball men declared, "the Sox would now have to win the flag."

Pools Protected, Charge

Mr. Johnson also disclosed that either powerful official or political circles are protecting baseball gambling pools. He said he hoped all lovers of baseball would help wipe out this condition by reporting all evidence of crookedness to the grand jury. He was anxious to find some method to get at the gamblers who are threatening to ruin the national game.

"I am determined that baseball shall be divorced from gambling and that the black sheep be driven out of the game," he declared. "The percentage of dishonest ballplayers is small, but we have some."

Various players in both major leagues, he said, "have walked the plank." He mentioned Chase, Lee Masec and Zimmerman.

Pass Tells of Losses

Although in the juryroom for an hour and a half, Samuel Pass said he had given no direct testimony. He had no facts, only hearsay, and he had entertained the jurors by telling funny stories about the players.

He told reporters he had been acquainted with White Sox players for about eight years. He was so confident they could not lose the 1919 world's series that he had wagered all his available money. He did not place any with known gamblers, but took all bets offered by persons he came in contact with.

He witnessed all the games, but nothing transpired that he could term suspicious.

Gives Hints to Jury

After the first game he asked Cicotte why he lost and Cicotte replied he was out of form. After Williams lost the second game he asked Williams the reason and was likewise told that he was out of form. In the succeeding games the players all showed poor form and admitted to him after each game that they could not "get their stride."

He said he made several suggestions which would help the grand jury in getting at the bottom of the rumors and hints that the World's title was tossed away by the Sox for the benefit of a gambling syndicate.

The grand jury investigation then was continued until Tuesday. As the jury ceases operations on Sept. 30, that leaves only three days to complete the inquiry. No indictments are expected.

FROM JAMES CRUSINBERRY, " 'BENTON CONFESSED WINNING $1,500 ON WIRE TIP'—HERZOG" (Chicago *Tribune*, September 24, 1920)

That "Rube" Benton, the New York Giants' pitcher, who is said to have won $3,800 on the world's series of 1919 after being tipped off by Hal Chase that the affair was "fixed" for Cincinnati to win, actually won $1,500, and said so in an affidavit now in the possession of President Heydler of the National league, was the statement made last night by Charles Herzog, Cub infielder, who in turn had been accused by Benton of offering him a bribe to "throw" a game late in 1919.

Benton, who arrived from New York yesterday and testified before the grand jury in its investigation of alleged crookedness in baseball, first declared to reporters that he hadn't bet at all on the series last fall. Later he told one reporter he had wagered a small amount in a café and handed it to the waiter. Still later, when asked pointedly regarding his betting on the series, he said he had wagered $20 on Cincinnati to win one of the games, and after winning the bet had spent the money over the bar in a New York saloon.

The alleged $1,500 winnings were disclosed by Herzog when he was told what his accuser had said regarding betting.

"I know Art Wilson and Tony Boeckel stated in their depositions that Benton had told them of winning about $3,800," said Herzog. "They made those depositions in May, while here in Chicago. It was in June, when Benton and myself were in President Heydler's office together, that the amount was named as $1,500. I was there when Benton named the amount in a sworn statement which Mr. Heydler has. Perhaps he will produce it when he appears before the grand jury next week.

"In his sworn statement Benton confessed to Heydler that he bet on the strength of a telegram he had received. That was the important point Mr. Heydler desired to bring out."

It was after his appearance before the grand jurors that Benton told of the $20 wager. He talked about [it] as follows:

"I remember being with Wilson, Boeckel, and McCarty in the Braddock hotel in New York, but I don't believe I said I had won any $3,800 on a tip from Hal Chase. I might have said something in a kidding way to Wilson and Boeckel.

"The only bet I made was one afternoon during the series in New York. Some one wanted to bet on the White Sox. I took the bet, $20, taking the Reds' end of it. When the game was over I laid the money on the bar and we drank it up."

Saw "Tipoff" Telegram

"Did you see any telegram indicating the thing was fixed?" Rube was asked.

"Yes, I did," was his answer. "I don't know who sent it, but it came to Jean Dubuc, who was barnstorming with us. It simply said: 'Bet on the Cincinnati team today.'

"I supposed it came from Bill Burns who had been close to Dubuc a few weeks before the series, when both were living at the Ansonia hotel in New York. Chase was getting telegrams, lots of them, just before and during the world's series. I didn't see them, but I am sure Hal was betting heavily on Cincinnati. I couldn't go on the witness stand and swear to it, but it is my belief he won as much as $20,000 on the series."

Burns Also Red Bettor?

The Bill Burns referred to by Benton is a former pitcher for Washington and other American league clubs.

When the world's series began he was in Cincinnati and traveled back and forth between Cincinnati and Chicago. He was supposed to be wagering heavily on the Cincinnati team to win. Burns now is said to be living somewhere in the southwest.

Herzog made no effort to see Benton yesterday, but was busy attempting to clear himself of the charge of trying to bribe the New York pitcher.

The manager and one of the assistant managers of Stillson's, when presented to Herzog, stated that to their knowledge they never had seen him before. Stillson's was the place named by Benton as the saloon where he thought the offer had been made.

FROM "INSIDE STORY OF PLOT TO BUY WORLD'S SERIES"
(Chicago *Tribune*, September 25, 1920)

Attel, Chase, Named in $100,000 Ring

The gamblers' inside story of the baseball bribe offer by which the last world's series is alleged to have been "thrown" by a coterie of White Sox players to the Cincinnati club, became public last night, substantially in the form in which it has been told to the Cook county grand jury.

The central figures in the story are the ones about whom the entire investigation of alleged crookedness in organized baseball centers.

According to the gamblers' account of the transaction, the amount actually paid to the White Sox players was $15,000, though more was promised.

Abe Attel a Go-Between

This story is as follows:

A few weeks before the close of the 1919 season, Abe Attel, the boxer, was approached at the Polo grounds in New York by Hal Chase, since retired from organized baseball, and asked whether he could find a gambler who would pay $100,000 to "fix" the world's series. The boxer agreed to put the proposition before Arnold Rothstein, a big New York operator.

Attel approached Rothstein with his plan and was chased from his office. This did not stop Attel, however, and after consulting friends he told Chase that Rothstein was agreeable and that everything was arranged.

Cut $100,000 Deal

The deal was for $100,000 in installments, $15,000 after the Sox lost the first game, $20,000 on the morning of the third day, $25,000 on the fourth morning and the balance after the series ended.

Chase made another appointment at which were present two Sox players to verify his statements.

After this Attel scurried around, forming a combination to place wagers, intending to have agents in every big city. Chase did the same; for he had no intention of giving Attel a monopoly of the good things, although that had been the understanding. Chase made deals with several big gamblers, including one known at New Orleans tracks, and subsequently warned away from that track.

Get Fixer for Players

When the series started, however, Chase could not go to Cincinnati. The season being over, he had picked a team of big league exposition players, who were on a barn-storming tour of the east. So a gobetween [*sic*] was engaged to act as intermediary for Attel and the Sox players who had agreed to "throw" the series.

Everything went according to schedule. Attel obtained backing and fairly swamped the country with money on Cincinnati against the Sox.

The Sox lost the first game, Cicotte pitching. Attel handed over $15,000 the next morning.

The second game also went to the Reds, Williams hurling. By this time Attel had visions of saving the remainder of the "pot" he had promised to pay, so he stalled when he met the Sox go-between in Chicago the third day. [This go-between's name is known to the grand jury.]

Backs Down on Payment

Attel exhibited a telegram from New York, which he had arranged to have sent, reading: "Money on way." The initials signed were similar to those of Rothstein. Attel kept the Sox go-between waiting almost to game time by explaining the telegraph office cashier was out to lunch and Attel could not get the money until after the game.

The Sox go-between fell for the alibi and meantime had to hurry out to the White Sox park, to see that all was right. Attel thought if the Sox lost the third game the Reds certainly could win two of the next five on their merits against the demoralized Sox, and that he would save the rest of the promised payment.

Sox Win; Gamblers Lose

Then came the only hitch in the whole plan. The fixers reckoned without Pitcher Kerr, who was not "in," and the Sox won the third game. The sure thing gamblers lost nearly all they had won on the first two games, but still had the bulk of their coin riding on the result of the series, which they won.

It had been agreed to prorate the cost, according to the amount placed, and Attel is said to have furnished $2,800 of the $15,000 paid. What Chase is alleged to have received from the other gamblers he let in on it is not known. He probably took all he could get, as in transactions of this kind there is always danger of the "double cross."

It was Attel's understanding that five White Sox players were in on the deal. Four [sic] members of the team were known to be honest, beyond question—two pitchers, two outfielders, and an infielder. Concerning the others, Attel had no information from Chase.

Hahn Disputes Benton

Before he left for New York yesterday "Rube" Benton, the Giant pitcher, stated that a "Cincinnati man named Hahn, a betting commissioner for a syndicate of gamblers," had told him the world's series last year was fixed for Cincinnati to win; that five Sox players, among them Cicotte, Gandil, Williams and Felsch, were to take pay for throwing games; and that the price was $100,000.

Hahn arrived in Chicago yesterday and made a complete denial of Benton's statements. He is Philip Hahn, a racetrack man. He read what Benton had to say and then went to Attorney Michael F. Ryan in the Transportation building and made two affidavits, one to be sent to the Cincinnati baseball team officials.

Didn't Bet a Nickel

He admitted he had been on a hunting trip in North Carolina with Benton. But he swore he is not and was not a betting commissioner; that he knows no gambling syndicate; that he didn't bet a nickel on the series, either for himself or anybody else; and that he doesn't know Cicotte, Gandil, Williams, or Felsch.

Moreover, he offers to give $5,000 to any charity the Tribune may name if it can be proved he had anything to do with the baseball scandal or had bet any money on the series.

Through his attorney he assured the state's attorney's office he would be in Chicago Tuesday, ready to go before the grand jury. Then he took a train for northern Wisconsin to go hunting.

Jury Gets More Time

The present grand jury will continue its investigation of alleged crookedness in organized baseball—particularly in the last world's series—if it takes another month. The jury's time is up next week, but according to Assistant State's Attorney Hartley Replogle, it will be retained as a special grand jury for the baseball case and can hold afternoon and evening sessions.

Several more players may be summoned—men of the New York and Brooklyn clubs who are said to have won money on the series "on sure fire tips." Gamblers from various cities—two big ones from New York especially—may be brought here to testify.

Call Chiefs of Giants

Mont Tennes, Jim O'Leary and many others have been mentioned as likely to be called to the state's attorney's office for questioning, and the promoters of baseball pools are under scrutiny.

John "Muggsy" McGraw and President Stoneham of the Giants have been summoned by the jury and may testify next week. The inquiry will be resumed Tuesday.

It developed yesterday that William Tennes, brother of Mont, was a constant companion of two star Cub players until the "scandal" broke; that one of the players has been under a cloud in connection with the

Philadelphia game the alleged fixing of which caused the investigation; and that Tennes had lost heavily on the world's series in 1919.

Eight Players' Pay Held Up

The names of various Sox players have been mentioned in connection with the charge that the world's championship was "thrown" to Cincinnati. Charles A. Comiskey has so far refused to make public the names of the players whose pay checks and bonuses were held up, but it has become generally reported that they are:

BUCK WEAVER, third baseman.

HAPPY FELSCH, center fielder.

CLAUDE WILLIAMS, pitcher.

CHARLES RISBERG, shortstop.

JOE JACKSON, left fielder.

CHICK GANDIL, first baseman.

EDDIE CICOTTE, pitcher.

FRED McMULLIN, utility player.

A woman's name was mentioned yesterday as that of a person being investigated by attachés of the state's attorney's office in connection with the world series gambling.

FROM "FIRST EVIDENCE OF MONEY PAID TO SOX BARED"
(Chicago Tribune, September 26, 1920)

McMullin's Mystery Package Trailed

Evidence purporting to show the actual passing of money to White Sox participants in the last world's series is ready for the grand jury—the first tangible clew to corruption.

This evidence concerns the delivery of a mysterious package in the shape of currency by Fred McMullin, White Sox utility man, to the home of Buck Weaver, Sox third baseman, during the playing of the world's series last fall, and will be investigated when the grand jury resumes its inquiry into crookedness in professional baseball on Tuesday.

• • •

The testimony of several witnesses last week laid the foundation for the probe of the mysterious package.

A new witness, a Chicago dentist who is said to do the dental work for the Weaver family, is now being sought by Assistant State's Attorney Hartley Replogle regarding the delivery of the package. The story already told the grand jury is that he heard the details of it from Weaver's mother-in-law, Mrs. Cook, who was said to have been present at Weaver's house when the delivery was made.

The report is that Weaver was out when McMullin called with the package; that after waiting a long time McMullin left the package and departed. When Weaver came home and learned what had happened, he is said to have stormed and refused to touch the thing, but later accepted it.

Package Stirs Suspicions

Just what the package contained never was learned, nor was it learned whether McMullin delivered packages to other Sox. If the proper witness is procured the mystery may be cleared up.

It was said that Weaver's action stirred suspicion among those who witnessed the incident, for even at that time there were whispered rumors of something being wrong with the world's series.

Weaver's Check Held Up

While McMullin didn't take an active part in the series as a regular, his name was linked with those under suspicion and he was among the eight whose bonus checks were withheld for several weeks after the series was over.

McMullin was sent to Cincinnati by Manager Gleason to spy on the Reds during the closing games of the regular season, just as the Reds had a man, Johnny Evers, to spy on the White Sox before the big series began. He was supposed to watch the Reds and report to Gleason their weaknesses and strong points.

Some of the rumors had it McMullin spent part of the time in other cities and that his reports on the Reds were incorrect in many instances. During the series, and ever since, McMullin has associated closely with the players now under suspicion.

Bring in Gandil and Burns

Reports yesterday mentioned McMullin's name in connection with those of eight players. It was also said that Chick Gandil, former first baseman, was "very close in his confidence." Bill Burns, ex-Sox pitcher, was named as the man who spread the tip in Chicago that Cincinnati was to win the series.

Pittsburgh gamblers who won hundreds of thousands of dollars on the series declared the money which was to be divided among the players was placed in the hands of one of McMullin's intimates before the games started. Abe Attel, the boxer, they said, wired before each game instructions on how the money was to be placed.

District Attorney Harry H. Rowand of Pittsburgh is making an investigation.

FROM JAMES CRUSINBERRY, "SOX SUSPECTED BY COMISKEY DURING SERIES"
(Chicago *Tribune*, September 27, 1920)

Sought Inquiry after First Defeat

Charles A. Comiskey, owner of the White Sox, admitted yesterday that he was convinced after the first game of the world's series last fall against the Cincinnati Reds that someone had "fixed" some of his players. His admission was verified and amplified by President John A. Heydler of the National league, who arrived in Chicago to testify before the grand jury tomorrow when the baseball investigation is renewed.

Comiskey took the matter up with Heydler the morning following the first game because he was not on speaking terms with President Ban Johnson of the American league and because Garry Herrmann, head of the National commission, was president of the Reds, the rival team. Comiskey also called Heydler into conference after the second game, more thoroughly convinced that certain White Sox players were trying to throw the games to Cincinnati.

Mont Tennes Ready to Appear

This disclosure, and a statement by Mont Tennes, prominent among big gamblers of Chicago, that he was ready and willing to go before the grand jury and tell anything he knows of betting on the 1919 series, were the day's important developments in the airing of professional baseball. That startling evidence will be presented when the investigation is resumed tomorrow seems certain.

Ban Johnson returned yesterday from New York, where he had a conference with Arnold Rothstein, wealthy race track man, whose name was connected with rumors of fixing the world's series.

Johnston [*sic*] stated he had been convinced Rothstein wasn't in on the frameup, but he said Rothstein admitted he knew about it.

Heydler's Story

Heydler told of his conferences with Comiskey during the series after he was assured the Sox owner had admitted the facts. Heydler referred to notes and papers which he has with him to present to the grand jury as evidence.

"Commy was all broken up and felt something was wrong with his team in that first game," Heydler said. "To me such a thing as crookedness in that game didn't seem possible. I told Comiskey I thought the White Sox were rather taken by surprise, that perhaps they had underestimated the strength of the Cincinnati team.

"The matter was dropped for the time. That day the Reds won again and we moved to Chicago for the third game. Comiskey called me on the telephone early that morning, and with John Bruce, secretary of the national commission, I went to his office at the ball park. Once more he stated he felt sure something was wrong.

Tells of "Coppered" Bet

"Still I couldn't believe it. Among other things he told of a Chicago fan who had gone to Cincinnati and wagered on the White Sox, but after getting some "inside" information from gambling friends this man had switched and wagered on Cincinnati.

"Comiskey said his manager, Kid Gleason, felt convinced some one had 'reached' the Sox players and that they had talked the matter over and felt an investigation should be made. I still believed he was mistaken, but I took the matter up with Ban Johnson later, at the game. Johnson replied with a rather curt remark that made me drop the matter.

"After the series an article appeared in one paper hinting that the series had been fixed. I went to Johnson and said the affair should be taken up and cleaned up at once. But Johnson agreed to investigate the affairs, and I thought it was really his case and that he would handle it correctly."

Comiskey Again Raps Johnson

Comiskey's admission of his suspicions following the first game came after yesterday's game at Sox park.

"There's one man working on this investigation who I did think was sincere in it, but I believe now he's using it for his own personal gain," Comiskey said. "It was a terrible thing to see a story printed of crookedness on the White Sox recently. Just before they went into a tough series against New York, but it was still worse to follow with a statement of blackmail of my players by gamblers just before they went into the series against Cleveland, a club in which this man is interested. I refer to Ban Johnson, president of our league.

"I started investigating last fall right after the series. I sent Manager Gleason and two other men to St. Louis to follow up a clew and Johnson followed by going down there and then saying that Gleason bungled the affair."

Herzog Seems Cleared

President Heydler indicated his testimony before the jury will clear all charges against Charley Herzog. His evidence gathered for the grand jury shows Rube Benton first stated positively that Herzog had offered him $800 to throw a ball game, then later declared he didn't know whether it was Herzog or Chase, and finally stated it was Chase.

Also it was determined that Benton had admitted in Heydler's office that he won $1,500 on the world's series last fall on the strength of a telegram, and that the telegram was from Bill Burns, not from Chase.

Heydler had visited Pittsburgh, Detroit, and Cleveland in an effort to obtain evidence of the "fixing" of the Cubs-Phillies game of Aug. 31, and stated he was convinced a tip had circulated among gamblers that the game was "fixed," but as yet he had been unable to produce any direct evidence.

"I'm sure the warnings sent to the Chicago club weren't sent by any friends of baseball," Heydler said. "I've heard so much about crookedness in baseball in the last year that I wouldn't say anything any more."

Fans Cheer Sox Players

Regardless of the suspicion cast upon some members of the White Sox they were loudly cheered by the fans yesterday at the south side game. Several players when seen last night, including Capt. Eddie Collins, Manager Gleason, and Ray Schalk, stated they will be glad to go before the grand jury and tell anything they know and answer any questions they can.

Fred McMullin, utility man, whose name was connected with a report of leaving a package in the shape of money at Buck Weaver's home during the last world's series, stated he had been to Weaver's home often but that he knew absolutely nothing about any packages that looked like money.

Mont Tennes, who Charles Weeghman, president and former owner of the Cubs, named as having declared the 1919 world's series "fixed" last night said he was willing to face a grand jury at any time.

"I'm willing," Mr. Tennes said, "to tell them all I know about baseball and betting on baseball—but I can tell them nothing about fixed games. I know nothing about fixed games.

"I never told Charley Weeghman about fixed games. Weeghman's intentions are good, I'm sure, but I believe he was misunderstood. Whether Weeghman and I met at Saratoga I can't say. I remember meeting him at a racetrack last summer. Of course we talked baseball—one would have to talk baseball with Charles. I told him I had bet, or intended betting on the White Sox. I don't remember which it was.

"I bet on the White Sox. I lost my bet, and I made no cry of fraud."

Assistant State's Attorney Hartley Replogle called off a special grand jury session set for tonight to hear the statements of certain ball players. Mr. Replogle explained that as the Sox victory yesterday left them in the pennant race he did not wish to handicap the team by calling any of its players. They will not be heard until after the season closes or after they are out of the race.

Mr. Replogle saw yesterday's game at the south side and conferred with Comiskey and Manager Gleason.

FROM "GRAND JURY TO HEAR 'MYSTERY' WOMAN'S STORY"
(Chicago *Tribune*, September 28, 1920)

Mrs. Kelley to Testify on Baseball Scandal

When the investigation of alleged crookedness in professional baseball is resumed today before the Cook county grand jury the star witness is expected to be Mrs. Henrietta D. Kelley. The "woman of mystery" in the baseball case was identified yesterday as a widow who owns furnished apartments at 3901 Grand boulevard, some of which at various times have been occupied by White Sox ball players, including Eddie Cicotte.

The testimony she has to offer will be something bearing directly on the alleged fixing of the world's series last fall, according to reports from the state's attorney's office. Mrs. Kelley, for years a White Sox fan as well as a close friend of many of the players who have been her tenants, was one of the host of rooters who went to Cincinnati last fall to see the first two games of the big series.

Sox Manager on Stand

That it will be a busy afternoon at the Criminal court building is assured. In addition to Mrs. Kelley other important witnesses have been called.

William "Kid" Gleason, manager of the White Sox, who suspected something was wrong with his team in the series last fall before the first game had been finished, is expected to tell of his efforts to trace rumors of crookedness in the series.

Eddie Collins, captain and second baseman of the White Sox, will be asked concerning several plays which occurred during the world's series with the Reds.

Ray Schalk, catcher of the Sox, will be asked concerning plays on the ball field that didn't look exactly right, and other things off the ball field that he observed.

John A. Heydler, president of the National league, will tell the jury about being informed by Comiskey after the first game of the series that the latter felt there had been some "fixing" of his ball players. Heydler also will present testimony concerning the charge of Rube Benton that Charley Herzog of the Cubs offered a bribe. The testimony and affidavits conflict with the statement given out here by Benton last week.

Was Hostess to Cicotte Family

At various times Eddie Cicotte, John Collins, and Roy Wilkinson have occupied apartments in Mrs. Kelley's building and among her friends are Eddie Collins and Ray Schalk. It was said that during the world's series Eddie Cicotte and his family were stopping in the private home of Mrs. Kelley as her guests, their lease on an apartment which they occupied during the regular season having expired. Jack Cicotte, Eddie's brother, was also a guest.

That Mrs. Kelley doesn't care to be exploited in the matter was evident yesterday at the final game of the season at the Sox park. A newspaper photographer attempted to take her picture while she was seated in a box near the Sox bench. She refused to allow the picture. Just as the game ended the photographer made another attempt, which riled her escort. The man leaped upon the field and slapped the photographer in the face then followed with a kick on the shins.

McGraw Due Today

John J. McGraw, manager of the New York Giants, is expected in Chicago today. He will be called before the jury, probably tomorrow.

Reports that Buck Weaver and Fred McMullin, Sox players, whose names are said to have been mentioned to the grand jury, had been refused a hearing were denied by Mr. Replogle. He also denied that sixteen major league teams had been implicated in gambling and throwing games in evidence already received.

"There are only one or two teams involved so far, and just a few players," he said.

THE TEAPOT DOME SCANDAL

In the minds of many people, the most shocking scandals of the twenties were the ones associated with the administration of President Warren Gamaliel Harding. These scandals first broke in 1924, and Fitzgerald used them as the basis for his play *The Vegetable*, in which a quite ordinary person dreams he is president and unintentionally creates a criminal catastrophe through his own incompetence and that of the family members he carries into office with him. The Harding administration does not figure openly in *The Great Gatsby*, but the feeling and mood these scandals created is very much a part of the novel and must be taken into account if it is to be understood as the complex work of art it is.

Harding had been an admired, beloved, and trusted president. Kind, personable, and handsome, he seemed a welcome change from the rigidity and standoffishness of his predecessor, Woodrow Wilson. Harding mixed with the people and opened the White House grounds to them in a way that Wilson had not. The entire country mourned when he died on August 2, 1923. Speakers everywhere praised him, and crowds all across the nation paid their respects as his funeral train passed.

But soon after his death the scandals surfaced. The formerly beloved Harding was now the subject of gossip and speculation. There were rumors that he had killed himself and even that his wife had poisoned him to spare him the agony of disgrace. These stories are almost certainly untrue. What probably *is* true is that Harding knew what was coming and that the tension aggravated his heart problem.

There were several scandals, but the most notorious and far-reaching was the Teapot Dome case. Oil reserves on public land had been leased to private oil companies under suspicious circumstances. A complicated series of investigations, charges, and countercharges over the next few years finally led to the conviction of Secretary of Interior Albert B. Fall on a charge of taking a bribe. Two oilmen, Harry F. Sinclair and Edward L. Doheny, were acquitted of paying the bribes. Sinclair, however, was later convicted on other charges growing out of the case. He was found guilty of contempt of Congress for refusing to answer questions before the

U.S. Senate Committee on Public Lands and Surveys and for hiring private detectives to follow members of a jury before which he was tried. Remember that this is corruption at nearly the top of American society. It could go no higher unless it involved the president himself. President Harding was not directly implicated in the scandal, but his name and that of his administration were tarnished forever.

Doheny testified before the U.S. Senate Committee on Public Lands and Surveys and a crowd of reporters and onlookers on January 24, 1924, when publicity over the Teapot Dome case was raging. Under Secretary of Interior Albert Fall, the Interior Department had leased federal oil lands to Harry Sinclair's Mammoth Oil Company (the Teapot Dome reserves in Wyoming) and to Doheny's Pan-American Petroleum and Transport Company (the Elk Hills reserves in California). It was eventually established that Fall had received major financial favors from both Sinclair and Doheny.

It has been argued quite seriously, as Doheny did before the Senate, that the government did not get a bad deal in this arrangement. But the most important issue was whether or not Doheny had bribed Fall. Doheny had lent Fall $100,000 in cash with no security given on November 3, 1921, several months before the leasing arrangements were made. Doheny, quite naturally, insisted that the loan was a personal matter and had nothing to do with the lease. He explained the nature of his contract with the government and stated that he won the contract by submitting the lowest bid. (Information like this could easily have been verified elsewhere.) Doheny's company was to build oil storage tanks for the government at Pearl Harbor and instead of being paid in cash was to be paid in crude oil from federal reserves.

Doheny's bid, however, also included an offer of an alternative contract. His company would sacrifice some of its profit from the construction work at Pearl Harbor in return for the right to draw oil from designated federal reserve fields. If the construction costs should be less than the estimates, these savings too would be passed on to the government. (The end result of this arrangement, although Doheny does not specifically say so, was that Pan-American Petroleum and Transport Company got exclusive rights to the Elk Hills reserves.)

Doheny said, quite correctly for the short term, at least, that his contract saved the government money. His bid was the lowest in the first place, and the alternative contract provided construction even more cheaply. An additional provision allowed the government to buy fuel oil for fifty cents less a barrel than it could otherwise have done.

Doheny read into the record a letter of April 25, 1922, to his company's attorney from the Acting Secretary of the Interior and the Secretary of the Navy. In its rather forbidding legalese, the letter accepts the alternative contract, stipulates the rate of royalties the government will receive on the oil, and designates areas where the company may drill. At first glance this whole transaction seems reasonable and aboveboard. This impression was reinforced when Doheny's attorney, Gavin McNab, offered to give up the contract if the government could find a better offer.

But let us examine the situation a bit more closely. There is no limit to the amount of oil the company can draw from these reserves. It is true that the government will get a royalty on whatever oil is drawn, but it is also true that one purpose of the reserves is to make sure that there will be oil available in case of war or other emergencies. The oil may now be entirely depleted.

It was one thing to use government oil to pay for construction of storage tanks. It was quite another to allow unlimited drilling. If the purpose was conservation, one might possibly make a case for using a portion of the reserves to pay for storage construction. But there is little to be said for paying for storage tanks by giving an oil company an unlimited right to draw oil out of a reserve area and sell it on the market. To someone with a business orientation and no interest in conservation, Doheny's contract might seem reasonable. To a conservationist it might seem a case of governmental stupidity or deliberate governmental connivance in sharp practice. If the contract itself was at best questionable, Doheny's loan to Fall was nearly impossible to defend. The loan was supposedly made out of compassion for an old friend, but if there was nothing suspicious about it, why was the loan made in cash carried in a black bag? Surely it would have been simpler to give Fall a check. Doheny squirmed a good deal at this point.

He was so rich, he said, that $100,000 was merely a small, casual sum to him. Why not just use cash? But one might ask whether he had ever written checks for $400 or $500. He claimed he had had to adjust his financial methods in Mexico by using cash because of a fear of "robbers." One must assume, supposedly, that he means dishonest financial and governmental institutions, but that is not made at all clear. In any case, what do conditions in Mexico have to do with a financial transaction in the eastern United States?

Moreover, Doheny had appeared before the same committee on December 3, 1923, and he had not mentioned the loan then (it is only fair to note that he had not been asked about it directly). Fall, for his part, had denied in a letter to the Senate that he had received anything from either Sinclair or Doheny. This, of course, was now proven to be a lie. Doheny's testimony made the prospects for himself and for Fall seem quite bleak. The Supreme Court eventually threw out the leases granted to both Doheny and Sinclair.

FROM THE TESTIMONY OF EDWARD L. DOHENY BEFORE THE
U.S. SENATE COMMITTEE ON PUBLIC LANDS AND SURVEYS
*(The Teapot Dome Documents: A Microfilm Project of University
Publications of America,* 1975, pp. 1771–75, 1778–82)

Doheny's Statement, January 24, 1924

I have been following the reports of the proceedings before your committee and have concluded that notwithstanding my authorization to former Secretary [Albert Fall] early in December to state the full and complete facts in connection with personal transactions had in 1921 between Mr. Fall and myself, Mr. Fall has been making an effort to keep my name out of the discussion for the reason that a full statement might be misunderstood.

Whether there is a possibility of such misunderstanding or not, I wish to state to the committee and to the public the full facts, and I may say here that I regret that when I was before your committee I did not tell you what I am now telling you.

I did not do so for the reason that such a statement was not pertinent in answer to any of the questions asked me by members of the committee and to have done so would have been volunteering something in no way connected with the contracts made with the Pan-American Petroleum and Transport Company.

When asked by your chairman whether Mr. Fall has profited by the contract, directly or indirectly, I answered in the negative. That answer I now reiterate.

I wish first to inform the committee that on the 30th day of November, 1921, I loaned Albert B. Fall $100,000 on his promissory note to enable him to purchase a ranch in New Mexico. This sum was loaned to Mr. Fall by me personally. It was my own money and did not belong in whole or in part to any oil company with which I am or have been connected. In connection with this loan, there was no discussion between Mr. Fall and myself as to any contract whatever.

This loan had no relation to any of the subsequent transactions. The transactions themselves in the order in which they occurred, dispose of any contention that they were influenced by my making a personal loan to a lifelong friend.

The reason for my making and Mr. Fall's accepting the loan was that we had been friends for more than 30 years. He had invested his savings for those years in his home ranch in New Mexico, which I understood was all that remained to him after the failure of mining investments in Mexico and nine years of public service in Washington, during which he could not properly attend to the management of his ranch.

His troubles had been increased in 1918 by the death of his daughter and his son, who, up to then, had taken his place in the management of his ranch.

In our frequent talks it was clear that the acquisition of a neighboring property controlling the water that flows through his home ranch was a hope of his amounting to an obsession. His failure to raise the necessary funds by realizing on his extensive and once valuable Mexican mine holdings had made him feel he was a victim of an untoward fate.

In one of these talks I indicated to him that I would be willing to make him the loan, and this seemed to relieve his mind greatly. In the autumn of 1921 he told me that the purchase had become possible by reason of the willingness of the then owners of the Harris ranch to sell and that the time had arrived when he was ready to take advantage of my offer to make the loan.

The lease on naval reserve No. 1 was the direct outgrowth of the contract which the Pan-American Petroleum and Transport Company made with the navy as a result of competitive bids, in which that company was the lowest bidder for the construction of certain storage facilities at Pearl Harbor, T[erritory of] H[awaii]. And in the absence of that contract the lease would never have been executed.

The Navy Department, through its representative, took up with us the question of constructing the improvements and facilities at Pearl Harbor and of paying for them with the royalty oil which the navy was then obtaining from the various leases in naval reserves Nos. 1 and 2, and of filling the tankage constructed with a large quantity of fuel oil.

I was entirely in sympathy with the purpose of the navy, the reasons for which have perhaps been better explained to your committee by the navy's representative, Admiral Robison, than I could hope to do. I promised Admiral Robison that our company would at least submit a bid to

perform the work under those conditions; that is, furnish the money to pay for the work of construction at the harbor and of filling the tanks with oil and receive in return royalty oil at the posted field price to the value of the money so expended. The incidents up to the date of the contract, and the fact that the contract was let on competitive bidding, eliminate any possibility of favor to the company by either the Navy Department or the Interior Department.

The negotiations for this contract between the Navy Department and the company were conducted by our local Washington attorney, who was assisted in determining the necessary calculations by our California general manager, who is president of the California company. As a result of their exchange of ideas, our California general manager decided that the terms of the proposed contract were not such as to be of any advantage to the company and that the company could not afford to take the risks attached to the performance of the contract for the conjectural profit that might result therefrom, and he so stated in a letter which he wrote to our Washington attorney.

Neither our Washington attorney nor our California general manager nor any other officer or attorney of the company had any knowledge of the loan which I made to Mr. Fall, that being an entirely private matter, involving in no way the company's funds.

When the bids were opened it was found that the bid of the Pan-American Petroleum and Transport Company was the lowest. The Washington attorney of the company had conceived the idea of making, in accordance with the provisions of the call for bids, in addition to an unqualified bid, an alternative bid showing a considerable saving to the government in the actual cost of the construction under the contract, and a recompense to the Pan-American Petroleum and Transport Company for such waiver of profit by giving it an opportunity later on to extend its petroleum business in California through the acquisition of additional oil territory whenever the navy might be disposed to make additional contracts for the development of its reserve.

The alternative bid was considered the most favorable by the representatives of the government as is shown by a letter addressed to the Washington attorney of the company under date of April 25, 1922, and signed in the absence of Mr. Fall from Washington by the Acting Secretary of the Interior and the Secretary of the Navy.

It follows:

In your proposals (A) and (B) of April 14, 1922, under each of which your bid was lowest received by the government, your company submitted two bids for the erection and construction of storage facilities at Pearl harbor, T. H., and the filling of these with fuel oil. In proposal (B) you offer to accept an amount of royalty crude

oil for fulfilling the contract, which, expressed in money, was
$235,184.40 less than the amount in proposal (A), and your com-
pany offered to give the government in addition any saving in the
cost of construction under the amount estimated, provided that the
government would give the company preferential right to lease certain lands in naval reserve No. 1 in California.

It is evident from our conversation of April 13 that your interpretation of preferential right was to the effect that the Pan-American
Petroleum and Transport Company desired the right to lease certain
specified lands in naval petroleum reserve No. 1, as well as preferential right to lease other land in naval petroleum reserve No. 1, to
the extent described in article 2 of contract. It is my understanding
from your conversation that unless the Pan-American Petroleum and
Transport Company could get a lease to certain lands, your company would not desire to enter into a contract under the terms
outlined in proposal (B) and preferred the government would accept proposal (A).

The Department of the Interior looks favorably upon proposal
(B) for the following reasons: (1) It provides for an immediate and
certain saving to the government of $235,184.40 over proposal (A).
(2) You suggest that it gives opportunity to effect an additional possible saving of a considerable amount should the contractor succeed
in erecting the storage facilities for less than the amount estimated.

It is my understanding that unless you secure definite assurance
from the department that your company would obtain leases for
certain tracts in naval reserve No. 1, the Pan-American Petroleum
and Transport Company would prefer not to enter into a contract
as outlined in proposal (B). In order that the government may take
advantage of a contract embodying the terms outlined in proposal
(B), I wish to advise you the Department of the Interior will agree
to grant to the Pan-American Petroleum and Transport Company,
within one year from the date of the delivery of a contract relative
to the Pearl Harbor project, leases to drill the following tracts of
land: The NE ¼ of Section 3, Tc1S, R24E, and the strip of land lying
in the east half of Section 34, T305, P24E, bounded on the east by
the tract of land to be leased to the Beiridge Oil Company.

The rate of royalty which the department will require in the two
tracts of land referred to above will not be greater than the following:

For all oil produced of less than 30 degrees Baume:

On that portion of the average production per well not exceeding
20 barrels per day for the calendar month, 12 ½ per cent.

On that portion of the average production per well of more than

20 barrels and not more than 50 barrels per day for the calendar month, 14 2/7 percent.

On that portion of the average production per well of more than 50 barrels and not more than 100 barrels per day for the calendar month, 16 ⅔ per cent.

On that portion of the average production per well of more than 100 barrels and not more than 200 barrels per day for the calendar month, 20 percent.

On that portion of the average production per well of more than 200 barrels and not more than 300 barrels per day for the calendar month, 25 per cent.

On that portion of the average production per well of more than 300 barrels and not more than 400 barrels per day for the calendar month, 30 per cent.

On that portion of the average production per well of more than 400 barrels per day for the calendar month, 35 per cent.

These facts conclusively demonstrate that there could not have been any collusion between the Pan-American Petroleum and Transport Company and anybody whomsoever.

The original contract provided for an expenditure by the company of $6,466,795.50 which amount reduced through economies made by the company in its construction work and its purchase of fuel oil by about $525,000 which, together with the sum of $235,000, the difference between the company's unqualified bid and its alternative bid, amounts to $750,000. To this might fairly be added the sum of $120,000 by which sum the company's unqualified bid was lower than its competitor's bid, thus making the contract an extremely advantageous one for the government, and as before stated, uncertain in its benefits to the company.

In addition, the government has received under a provision of the contract, the benefit of a decline of 50 cents per barrel in the purchase of fuel oil furnished it, amounting to about $725,000. The construction work under this contract is practically completed and the fuel oil has been delivered into the tanks at Pearl Harbor.

Later in the year 1922, and nearly a year after I had made the loan to Mr. Fall, the Navy Department, desiring additional storage facilities and petroleum products at Pearl Harbor, requested that the original contract of the Pan-American Petroleum and Transport Company be supplemented or that a new contract be made providing for the additional work and supplies, as is shown by the letter of the Secretary of the Navy dated November 29, 1922. For some time negotiations were carried on in which the president of our California company who came to Washington for that purpose, together with our Washington attorney, discussed all phases of the proposed supplemental arrangements with the representatives of the Navy and the Interior departments.

On the last day before the contract was signed, the president of the California company absolutely turned down the contract, stating that he believed there was [*sic*] no adequate benefits commensurate with the great risks assumed by the advancement on the part of the company of the necessary millions to pay the contractors who were to perform the construction work at Pearl Harbor and to furnish the petroleum products required. The estimated expenditure to be made under this supplemental contract for tankage facilities and petroleum products is $9,017,000, about one-half for petroleum supplies and one-half for storage facilities. The work is well under way and about $1,000,000 has been expended by the company on it.

This contract gave the navy just that service from the naval reserves that the Navy Department, through its acting engineer head, desired, which was immediate availability of its anticipated productions, delivered where the navy wanted it, in such quantities as were needed, and of the character and quality which the navy's requirements called for.

In addition, a burden, the advantage of which to the navy can scarcely be measured, was assumed by the company, that of providing for the navy in southern California 1,000,000 barrels of free oil storage, and of devoting 3,000,000 barrels of the company's Atlantic seaboard storage to the holding of that quantity of fuel oil subject to the navy's call for any time for a period of fifteen years.

The contract also gave the option to the navy of purchasing at the company's terminal station at San Pedro such petroleum supplies as the navy may require at 10 per cent below the market price.

In closing, I wish to state that I left Los Angeles on January 17 to come to Washington to present a statement of all the facts to the committee, and having been informed that Mr. Fall was in New Orleans took that route in order to apprise him of my intentions and found him already in entire accord with my purpose.

Doheny's attorney, Gavin McNab of San Francisco, then read a letter to the Senate committee. The letter, authorized by Doheny, suggested that the president appoint a board to examine the contracts the government held with Pan-American Petroleum and Transport Company. If the board concluded that the government's contracts were not the best possible, Doheny would ask his board of directors to "reconvey to the government all interest in such contracts," receiving only compensation for work performed.

To this point, Doheny's testimony had not hurt him. But then Senator Thomas Walsh pinned him down about the loan, the way it was made, and its probable influence on the contract he received.

Mr. Doheny—Furthermore, I studied law at the same time that Senator Fall did. I practiced for a short time in the same district that he did. I watched his career all through the development of it, as District Attorney, United States Judge and United States Senator. I was very much interested in him on account of our old associations. I, myself, followed prospecting. I was fortunate and accumulated quite a large amount of money. Senator Fall was unfortunate, and when he was telling me about his misfortunes, and at a time when it was coupled with his misfortune of having to bear the loss of his two children, two grown children, I felt greatly in sympathy with him. He was telling me about his hope of acquiring this ranch, and being of an impulsive nature I said to him:
"Whenever you need some money to pay for that ranch I will lend it to you."
He spoke to me at that time about possibly borrowing it from Ned McLean. And he said something at that time about giving the ranch as security. I said:
"I will lend it to you on your note. You do not need to give the ranch as security."
That relieved Senator Fall greatly. Later on he telephoned me that the time had come when the ranch could be purchased. When he telephoned to me about it I sent him the money. Whether he asked for the money in the form that I sent it, or whether I sent it in that form of my own election, I do not know. But I sent it in cash.
Senator Walsh—This conversation was some three or four weeks before that?
Mr. Doheny—Yes sir; I think so, at least three or four weeks prior to that time. It may not have been quite that long before, but it was about that time.
Senator Walsh—How soon after the telephone talk in which it was agreed between you that you could loan him the money? Did you actually send it to him?
Mr. Doheny—I sent it to him right away, I think the next day, or within a couple of days.
Senator Walsh—From New York to Washington?
Mr. Doheny—Yes, sir.
Senator Walsh—And the note then came back to you?

Mr. Doheny—Yes, sir, the note was brought back to me.

Senator Walsh—How did you transmit the money to him?

Mr. Doheny—In cash.

Senator Walsh—How did you transport the cash?

Mr. Doheny—In a satchel. The cash was put up in a regular bank bundle and taken over and delivered to him.

Senator Walsh—Who acted as your messenger in the matter?

Mr. Doheny—My son.

Senator Walsh—Where did you get the cash?

Mr. Doheny—I got the cash from the bank: from Blair & Co's bank in New York.

Senator Walsh—And how did you get it from the bank?

Mr. Doheny—I cashed a check.

Senator Walsh—Have you got the check?

Mr. Doheny—The check I can also send you. I saw the check just before I left.

Senator Walsh—Will you send that to the committee also?

Mr. Doheny—Yes, sir, and I can also, if you like, bring over the individuals in the bank who paid over the money to my son.

Senator Walsh—How did you come to make this remittance to Senator Fall in cash?

Mr. Doheny—That is just what I said a moment ago. I do not remember whether it was the result of his request or whether it was my own idea of sending it to him in cash to pay for the property. But he was going to use it down in New Mexico, and I thought, perhaps—well, I do not know exactly how that was, as my memory is not good on that point.

Senator Walsh—You are a man of very large affairs and of great business transactions, so that it was not unusual for you to have large money transactions, perhaps, but it was, was it not, an extraordinary way of remitting money?

Mr. Doheny—I do not know about that. But if you wish to ask me on that score, while they relate to a good many things that have no connections with this at all, yet I will say I think I have remitted more than a million dollars in that way in the last five years. It was not an unusual thing, due to the fact that we were doing business on a large scale in Mexico, and there we are held up by every band of robbers in Mexico that we meet up with, and in fact we are now being held up by a band of Huerta's forces.

Senator Walsh—I was not speaking of Mexico. I dare say that a remittance to Mexico would require that it be made in essentially a different way than in this country. But I am speaking of a remittance from New York to Washington.

Mr. Doheny—Well, it was not unusual in my business, Senator Walsh, to make a remittance in that way. And I might say here that in making the decision to lend this money to Mr. Fall I was greatly affected by his extreme pecuniary circumstances, which resulted, of course, from a long period, a lifetime of futile efforts. I realized that the amount of money I was loaning him was a bagatelle to me; that it was no more than $25 or $50 perhaps to the ordinary individual. Certainly a loan of $25 or $50 from one individual to another would not be considered at all extraordinary, and a loan of $100,000 from me to Mr. Fall is no more extraordinary.

Senator Walsh—I can appreciate that on your side, but looking at it from Senator Fall's side it was quite a loan.

Mr. Doheny—It was indeed, there is no question about that. And I am perfectly willing to admit that it probably caused him to have such a feeling that he would have been willing to favor me, but under the circumstances he did not have a chance to favor me. He did not carry on these negotiations. That is the point I would like for you to understand; that Senator Fall in my opinion was not influenced in any way by this loan, because the negotiations were carried on by men who were not under his control.

Senator Walsh—When did the negotiations commence which eventuated in the contract of April 25, 1922?

Mr. Doheny—I do not know. I think they commenced along in February. I was not so familiar with them. It was when we were requested to make a bid. It might have been as late as March, 1922.

Senator Walsh—There is some evidence here to the effect that the negotiations for that contract and the negotiations for the Sinclair contract ran along together.

Mr. Doheny—Well, that is not true. I do not think they did, Senator, notwithstanding the testimony here, as I remember the situation.

Senator Walsh—If I remember correctly Senator Fall gave testimony subsequently to that effect.

Mr. Doheny—I am still of the opinion that there were no negotiations on our part; that we simply put in our bids when the request for bids came out.

Senator Walsh—Wait a minute. The request for bids, in the first place, resulted in your contract of June, 1921, for the drilling of twenty-two offset wells?

Mr. Doheny—Yes, sir.

Senator Walsh—And you were operating under that contract during the month of June or July, 1921, and from that time on, were you not?

Mr. Doheny—Yes, sir.

Senator Walsh—So that [at] the time these negotiations were carried on resulting in the loan, you were operating under that contract?

Mr. Doheny—Under the contract of June?

Senator Walsh—Yes.

Mr. Doheny—Yes, sir.

Senator Walsh—And that was made upon competitive bids?

Mr. Doheny—Yes sir; and so was the contract of April 25, 1922.

Senator Walsh—Now, then, the department again called for bids for the construction of storage tanks at Pearl Harbor. And with respect to that you submitted two bids, as I understand from your statement?

Mr. Doheny—Yes, sir, simultaneously.

Senator Walsh—One of which conformed to the proposals?

Mr. Doheny—Yes, sir.

Senator Walsh—And the other conforming to the proposal, but offering a reduction in the amount and a compensatory feature giving you the preference right to the lease if the department should conclude to lease?

Mr. Doheny—Yes.

Senator Walsh—Well, of course, it was open to the department to accept either one of these bids it saw fit, you having tendered them, was it not?

Mr. Doheny—I think so. I still want to insist that I did not know anything at all about this Pearl Harbor contract until some time along in January, February or March, 1922. That is, as to the Pearl Harbor contract I am speaking of now.

Senator Walsh—Yes, I am speaking about that contract. But when you speak, Mr. Doheny, about it being impossible to favor you in connection with the matter, the department was at liberty to take either one of your proposals.

Mr. Doheny—Yes; and Mr. Finney decided that this was the proposal to take.

Senator Walsh—Was the one he would like to take?

Mr. Doheny—Yes, sir, and the Secretary of the Navy agreed with him in accordance with the letter he sent to us deciding upon the second proposal.

Senator Walsh—What was the conversation you had with Senator Fall anterior to your making the loan concerning his efforts to raise money?

Mr. Doheny—He was not making any efforts to raise money. He was just telling me of his hopes, that he wanted to buy this ranch,

and how he had expected to borrow the money or to get Ned Mc-
Lean, I think it is Ned McLean, to advance the money and take the
ranch as security, or something of that sort. I thought to myself that
was a hint to me if I wanted to so take it, and I took it very gladly
and said to him that I would loan him the money.

Senator Walsh—Yes, but Mr. Doheny, I understood your statement to contain the assertion that Senator Fall had failed to raise
the money on his Mexican properties.

[Later Doheny was questioned about Fall's personal involvement.]

Senator Walsh—Mr. Doheny, you knew at that time, of course,
that Senator Fall was charged with the administration of all the oil
lands of this country in the public domain?

Mr. Doheny—Yes.

Senator Walsh—And that the power of disposing of the naval
reserves had practically been assigned to him by Executive order?

Mr. Doheny—Well, I don't believe I knew about that, though I
may have known about it. I don't disclaim any knowledge of it.

Senator Walsh—Now did your company hold at that time any
leases on the public domain outside of the naval reserves?

Mr. Doheny—Yes, sir; we held the lease on Section 6, adjoining
the naval reserve, that we got from the Interior Department.

Senator Walsh—When did you get that lease?

Mr. Doheny—We got that lease—I got that—from John Barton
Payne. Mr. McNab, my attorney, assisted us in getting it. And with
regard to that, I don't know anything Senator, because I want to
say to you that the remark you made a while ago is perfectly true.
There is nothing extraordinary about me. I am just an ordinary, old-
time, impulsive, irresponsible, improvident sort of prospector, and
I do not pretend to keep track of the details of our business. This
particular business—I don't even know the Secretary from whom
we got Section 6, and I never saw the documents through which
we got it. They were arranged by Mr. Anderson in conjunction with
Mr. McNab. Mr. Anderson is my brother-in-law and general manager
of my property in California, a very astute man, the best judge of
oil lands that I know of in the State of California; and the reason I
am telling you that particular thing is that the fact that he was dis-
gusted with these two contracts and found fault in my agreeing to
them showed that there could not have been any collusion, because
he wouldn't have given a 5-cent piece for them. That is only corroborative evidence. In this Section 6 Mr. Anderson assisted Mr.
McNab in acquiring it.

NIGHTCLUB LIFE

When Fitzgerald mentions the Swastika Holding Company in chapter 9 of *The Great Gatsby*, he is reminding his readers of two colorful Prohibition figures, Larry Fay and Texas Guinan. Larry Fay considered the swastika his special lucky emblem because it appeared on the blanket of a horse on which he had bet and won at odds of one hundred to one. The winnings were the beginning of a career which included bootlegging, running a fleet of taxicabs that as a sideline transported liquor, and operating a series of nightclubs. His first club, in partnership with Texas Guinan, who was perhaps the most famous nightclub hostess of the 1920s, was decorated with a huge swastika, and swastikas appeared on his taxicabs.

Fay's tastes were expensive and garish. He once brought twelve trunks of clothes back from London. (Think of Gatsby showing his dozens of shirts to Daisy Buchanan.) He was said to have spent $75,000 decorating one of his clubs, a princely sum in those days. Because of the violence of his world he wore a bulletproof vest beneath his expensive shirts. One day in 1934 he neglected to wear it and was shot to death by the doorman of one of his own clubs. Fay had quarreled with him and because of Depression hard times had cut the man's salary in half.

Fay was well known on Broadway, but his partner Texas Guinan was nationally famous. After some successes as a silent screen heroine and musical comedy star, she found her calling as a wildly flamboyant hostess of nightclubs, beginning in 1923. At a typical Guinan club, the real action usually did not begin until past midnight and sometimes not until three A.M. (the curfew time) and then roared on until five in the morning.

Guinan greeted customers by shouting "Hello, Sucker!" and proceeded to sell them artificial champagne (aerated cider) at twenty-five dollars a bottle. Bear in mind that a dollar then was worth more than ten dollars today. She jokingly flirted with the customers, as did her troop of attractive girls, and maintained a pitch of excitement throughout the night. The girls were carefully supervised, however, and there was no sexual involvement.

Guinan was arrested so often on various charges that her arrests became a joke. She never underwent more than the briefest of incarcerations. She at times had the band strike up "The Prisoner's Song" when she was arrested, and she had a chain of golden padlocks made for herself. Once when she was arrested for selling liquor, the club customers followed her to the police station, singing "The Prisoner's Song" and blocking traffic. After her acquittal she starred in a musical comedy called *Padlocks of 1927*. This show greatly increased her following.

A national celebrity, she became friends with the equally famous evangelist Aimee Semple McPherson. When McPherson visited Guinan's clubs, she was invited to speak, and Guinan countered by appearing at McPherson's religious service and, on invitation, sang hymns. Finally police harassment and the hostility of the powerful gangster Dutch Schultz drove her from New York nightclubs.

According to rumor, she had told columnist Walter Winchell that Schultz had imported gunmen to kill rival gangster Vincent Coll, and Winchell had broken the story the night before Coll was riddled with a submachine gun while standing in a phone booth. Winchell used Coll's name but quite naturally did not use Schultz's, and officially the crime was unsolved. Eventually Schultz too would be murdered.

The following articles about Guinan's activities in 1927 appeared in the *New York Times*, where the fascinated public could follow the case in almost daily installments. Guinan defended herself against the charges in this case in the usual way, saying she was merely an employee and therefore could not be held responsible if the club violated the curfew. For the same reason she could not be held for contempt if the club opened in spite of an injunction against her. Her lawyers did their best to question the reliability of prosecution witnesses, and technically the injunction was faulty anyway because she did not operate or own the club. (The curfew for clubs was 3 A.M. This was about the time Guinan's clubs really became lively.) No one could prove that she sold liquor herself or prove that she knew it was being sold despite the fact that agents repeatedly saw that sales and other activities were signaled by a nod of her head. *The Great Gatsby* was published before these events took place but the newspaper coverage included here typifies the well-publicized antics of glamorous lawbreakers like those depicted in the novel. (Notice differences in detail between the accounts of February 17 and February 18.)

FROM "TEXAS GUINAN JAILED IN DRY RAID ON CLUB"
(*New York Times*, February 17, 1927)

"Texas" Guinan, one of Broadway's best known night club hostesses, and three of her "300 Club" employes at 151 West Fifty-fourth Street, were arrested and locked up in the West Forty-seventh Street Station early today after a dozen Federal prohibition agents had raided the club. It is alleged that three of the agents had spent many hours in the club last night and early today making merry and openly buying liquor.

The raid was made a little before 3 o'clock this morning, the night club curfew hour, when the club was crowded with men and women, while the orchestra was in full blast and Miss Guinan's entertainers were disporting on the dance floor. A dozen of the entertainers, some of them scantily clad, with fur coats thrown over their shoulders, and more than a hundred guests piled into taxicabs and followed the prohibition agents, the hostess and her three employes to the station house.

While those who could crowded into the narrow confines in front of Lieutenant Bernard McGowan's desk, the others milled around on the sidewalk and John W. Inglesby, head of the padlock division of the prohibition men, made his charge against the prisoners.

Two Charges Against Her

Miss Guinan was charged with violation of the national prohibition act in having and selling liquor, and then an additional charge of contempt of court was lodged against her because a personal injunction had been issued against her after her place was raided some time ago.

The other prisoners, Henry Littwin, 111 West 111th Street; John Golden, 1,140 President Street, Brooklyn, and Charles Miller, 890 Fox Street, the Bronx, were all charged with acting in concert.

Three agents spent some time in the club before they were able to establish a clear line of communication with what they declare was the source of supply of liquor. Then, they charge, they bought a pint of alleged whisky for $10.

This was the cue for the raid. One of the three inside slipped out, gave a signal to the other agents outside, and the party made a dash for the place. Littwin, the doorman, tried to prevent their entry but one agent drew his pistol and ordered him to one side. Littwin obeyed and the agents entered, walked up to where Miss Guinan sat on a high chair with a clapper in her hand and informed her she was under arrest.

The woman, who is noted along Broadway for her "wise cracks," rose to the occasion.

"What, again?" she said. "I hope I can ride in a taxi."

This courtesy was accorded her, and throwing a wrap over her evening gown she walked out to the street with Agent Inglesby by her side. Her entertainers did not wait for any signal, but they, too, seized their wraps and followed on behind.

Meanwhile the other agents had taken Golden, who is alleged to have sold the liquor to them; Miller, another waiter, and Littwin, the doorman, and they were driven to the station house.

Patrons Go Along, Too

The raid and arrests added an unexpected thrill to the night club patrons, and most of them, determined not to miss anything of the evening's show, trailed along in the rear.

When the question of bail was broached at the police station Agent Inglesby told Lieutenant McGowan that no bail would be permitted unless the order was signed by a Federal Judge. As she was being taken away Texas Guinan was asked if she wanted anything to read. She replied: "Yes, give me a couple of Confessionals; they'll make good reading for me."

FROM "TEXAS GUINAN HELD IN CELL NINE HOURS"
(New York Times, February 18, 1927)

Texas Guinan, hostess and entertainer at the Three Hundred Club, 151 West Fifty-fourth Street, which Federal prohibition agents raided early yesterday morning, was released in $1,000 bail shortly before noon by Federal Judge William Bondy. The acceptance of the bail bond by Judge Bondy released Miss Guinan from a cell in the West Thirtieth Street Police Station, where she had been held for nine hours on charges of illegal sale and possession of liquor and violation of a personal Federal injunction.

Although Miss Guinan will not be called to answer the charges growing out of yesterday morning's raid until next week, she is scheduled to appear this morning before Judge Bondy in the Federal Building in padlock proceedings against the Three Hundred Club. Evidence on which this action is based was obtained by Federal prohibition agents some time ago, and this, it was explained by Assistant United States Attorney Lowell W. Wadmond, is a separate case against the Three Hundred Club and those active in its management.

Denies She Violated Injunction

Michael Edelstein, representing the Three Hundred Club and its hostess, who appeared in the bail bond proceedings before Judge Bondy, declared that Miss Guinan is not the owner of the club and therefore cannot be charged with contempt for violation of any injunction issued against the club. He added that Miss Guinan had never been personally served with any injunction and could not be held liable for such violation.

Major Chester P. Mills, Federal prohibition administrator in the New York district, maintained that Miss Guinan is known as owner of the Three Hundred Club. He said yesterday afternoon that the charges of violating the Volstead act and violation of the Federal injunction will be pressed against Miss Guinan.

Major Mills denied yesterday published reports that one of the agents raiding the Three Hundred Club was the son of a Philadelphia millionaire who was angered by the loss of $7,000 in a round of the night clubs and joined the prohibition enforcement forces. Major Mills said the agent who alleges that he purchased a pint of liquor in the club for $10 and was responsible for the raid was one of the regular agents. He revealed that this agent is taking a law course during the day and works as a prohibition enforcement agent at night.

The three other agents taking part in the raid, according to Major Mills, have been members of the enforcement staff for four years or longer. He said each of these agents is dependent for a livelihood on his salary from the Government.

Says No Woman Went Along

Major Mills said only one agent wore evening clothes. He said none was accompanied to the Three Hundred Club by a woman. The raiding party was under the command of Captain John W. Inglesby, a veteran of the prohibition service.

Four employes of the club, arrested with Miss Guinan, were arraigned before United States Commissioner Garrett W. Cotter in the Federal Building on charges of possessing and selling liquor and were released under $500 bail each for a further hearing. They described themselves as Charles Miller, 32 years old of 890 Fox Street, the Bronx, manager of the Three Hundred Club; John Golden, 38, of 1,140 President Street, Brooklyn, a waiter; John Hagen, 38, of 417 West Forty-seventh Street, doorman, and Harry Litwin, 31, of 111 West 111th Street, starter.

FROM "PADLOCK ORDERED FOR THE 300 CLUB"
(New York Times, February 19, 1927)

The Three Hundred Club, raided by prohibition agents early Thursday morning, was ordered padlocked for six months by Federal Judge Bondy yesterday. The management consented to the decree, which will be put into effect in a few days. But Texas Guinan, who was arrested in the raid, escaped without a personal injunction being issued against her.

The United States Attorney's office insisted that yesterday's action would have no effect on its plans to bring Miss Guinan up for contempt of court as a result of Thursday's raid, the sale of liquor in the club having been forbidden by injunction previously, and scoffed at the contention that Miss Guinan's evasion of the personal injunction weakened the contempt charge against her.

The one thing that remains quite certain is that Miss Guinan must appear before United States Commissioner Cotter this morning with waiters from the club to plead to a new charge of violating the prohibition law, also growing out of Thursday's raid.

Miss Guinan Never Punished

Miss Guinan is a veteran of half a dozen raids and four padlock decrees, extending over three years. Yet she has never been long out of business, and has never personally suffered either fine or imprisonment.

The secret of Miss Guinan's successful operations, the authorities say, is that she is always "an innocent, if not victimized, employee." She is said to be financially interested in night club enterprises, and derives income from that source apart from salary. The Government has not established any financial interest or part ownership.

The Three Hundred Club was supposed to be Miss Guinan's own venture. It was opened last Spring on her return from Florida. The club was raided last July, but the cases against all the prisoners were dismissed. Last December agents are alleged to have gathered evidence of liquor sales in the club and as a result it was included in the list of places on which injunction papers were served in the Christmas raids.

Immediately after those raids a temporary injunction restraining the corporation and all its officers from further violations was issued. Miss Guinan was named in that injunction, a copy of which was posted on the premises, but she was never personally served with a copy by the United States Marshall.

Contempt Charge to Be Pressed

It is on that injunction, alleging that she was an officer of the corporation, or interested in it, that the contempt charge is to be pressed by the Government. The padlock injunction and personal injunction against Hyman Edson, issued yesterday, were the final disposition of that case.

Miss Guinan's lawyers say that the final disposition of the case failed to sustain the contention that Miss Guinan was financially interested in the club. Had she been a part owner, it is contended, she would have received a personal injunction with Mr. Edson. M. M. Edelstein, her counsel, objected to Assistant United States Attorney Wadmond's demand that she receive such an injunction, explaining to the Court that she was neither owner, part owner, nor manager of the club. The Court sustained Mr. Edelstein.

FROM "TEXAS GUINAN DISAPPOINTS"
(*New York Times*, February 20, 1927)

Fails to Plead to Liquor Charge, but Will Appear Tomorrow

Texas Guinan failed to appear before United States Commissioner Cotter yesterday morning to plead to a charge of violating the prohibition law growing out of the raid on the 300 Club early on Thursday morning. M. M. Edelstein, her attorney, said he had not thought her personal appearance would be necessary and gave the inclement weather as an excuse for her absence.

Commissioner Cotter postponed the pleading until Monday, and Mr. Edelstein promised to have his client in court then. Hearing on the case has been set for next Thursday.

Prohibition Agent Charles Smith told Commissioner Cotter that the man who had given his name as Charles Miller when arrested with Miss Guinan was really Hyman Edson, her manager, on whom a personal injunction had been served by order of Federal Judge Bondy on Friday. It was said afterward that the identification, if proved, would make Hyman liable for contempt of court for violating the previous temporary injunction against the 300 Club in which he was named.

FROM "TEXAS GUINAN FREED IN BAIL"
(*New York Times*, February 22, 1927)

Pleads Not Guilty on Charge of Maintaining a Nuisance

Texas Guinan, hostess at the 300 Club, 151 West Fifty-fourth Street, pleaded not guilty before United States Commissioner Garrett W. Cotter yesterday to a charge of maintaining a nuisance. She was released in $1,000 bail for a hearing Thursday.

M. Michael Edelstein entered the plea for Miss Guinan and handed Mr. Cotter the $1,000 bail bond. Then the defendant was ordered to the bar and told that she had been charged with maintaining a nuisance in West Forty-fourth Street.

"It's West Fifty-fourth Street," she corrected.

After she had sworn that she had "executed the bond for the purposes set forth therein," Miss Guinan started for the reporters' room on the fifth floor to hold what she called an "impromptu reception." As she got out of the elevator she struck her head against the top of the door.

"Well," she laughed, "looks as if they're trying to get rid of me before they get me in jail."

With Miss Guinan was her brother, Tommy. It was said by another man who accompanied her that she would be hostess in a new club within a few days.

FROM "TEXAS GUINAN'S CLUB CLOSED FOR SIX MONTHS"
(*New York Times*, February 24, 1927)

Padlock Is Snapped on the '300' for Dry Law Breach—Rival Seeks Its Patrons

At 5 o'clock yesterday afternoon Captain John Inglesby, Chief of the Padlock Division of the Prohibition Enforcement Staff, snapped a padlock which will interrupt for six months the career of Texas Guinan's Three Hundred Club at 151 West Fifty-fourth Street.

The actual padlocking was unannounced and was done so quietly that neither persons living nor working in the neighborhood nor the police of the West Forty-seventh Street Station had heard of it last night.

Shortly before theatre closing time patrons of the club drove up and expressed surprise at finding the place dark and a sign in one window announcing that it had been closed for violation of the Federal Prohibition act.

Another enterprising night club in the vicinity attempted to attract to its own doors the disappointed patrons of the Three Hundred Club. To all those who drove up to the darkened building a man stationed outside handed pamphlets describing the attractions of the rival establishment.

Before the padlocking Miss Guinan removed all the furnishings of her club.

FROM "GUINAN HEARING DELAYED"
(*New York Times*, February 25, 1927)

Dry Agents Fail to Appear in Court—Liquor Called "Synthetic"

Texas Guinan's hearing on a charge of selling liquor, made after the recent raid of the Three Hundred Club, was postponed yesterday by United States Commissioner Cotter until today because of the absence of Prohibition Agents Longcope and Fowler.

Miss Guinan was present. M. M. Edelstein, her attorney, objected to the postponement, contending that his client was entitled to an immediate hearing.

The report of the Government chemist on the pint of liquor alleged to have been seized in the raid on the Three Hundred Club, made to Prohibition Administrator Mills yesterday, described it as "synthetic Scotch, artificially colored, and made from redistilled denatured alcohol."

FROM "TEXAS GUINAN HELD ON NUISANCE CHARGE"
(*New York Times*, February 26, 1927)

Liquor Selling Accusation Is Dropped—Club Manager and Waiter Have Like Fate

LESSER DEFENDANTS FREED

Law Student Dry Agent Says He Purchased Whiskey—Another Supports Story

Texas Guinan was held for trial on the charge of maintaining a nuisance at the Three Hundred Club, after a three-hour hearing before United States Commissioner Cotter yesterday afternoon. A charge of selling liquor, which had been added to the original complaint, was dismissed.

Hyman Edson, alleged to be the manager of the club, and John Golden, waiter, by whom the sale of liquor in the club was alleged to have been made, were held with Miss Guinan. The charges against Harry Litwin, cab starter, and John Hogan, doorman, were dismissed.

Miss Guinan was reported to have been about to leave for a vacation in Havana. Her present status as defendant on a criminal charge, out on bail, will prevent her from leaving the jurisdiction of the Court unless she obtains special permission from the Court.

Assistant United States Attorney Meade Treadwell presented the Government's case against the defendants. The purchase of a pint of alleged whiskey from Golden was described by Prohibition Agent Truman Fowler. He said he bought it before the recent raid on the club. Fowler and J. Walter Longcope, another agent, who was in the club at the time, gave corroborative testimony.

M. M. Edelstein, attorney for the defendants, cross-examined Fowler and Longcope at length in an effort, he said, to attack their credibility. Fowler said he was employed last October, was a New York University law student working his way, rarely was in night clubs before his employment as an agent and had parents living in New Jersey. At one time

Edelstein accused Fowler of perjury, and the agent, who appeared extremely youthful, merely continued to answer questions, in some cases repeated twenty times.

Longcope, whose appearance indicated a person more at home on Broadway than Fowler, revealed under Mr. Edelstein's questioning that he had been employed as a newspaper reporter on various papers before he became an agent last month. Longcope was quoted at length in newspaper interviews following the raid, and was then said to be a member of a rich family who had lost much money in going the rounds of Broadway and had become an agent to "get even." Major Chester P. Mills, Prohibition Administrator, announced yesterday that Longcope would not be discharged, although he had unquestionably "spoken out of turn."

Thomas Miley, another agent, who testified to a previous purchase of liquor at the club, told of hearing Miss Guinan address a patron, "Sit down sucker," and order a waiter not to "let that one get out till his check is $50." Miley's testimony was directed toward showing Miss Guinan's authority on the premises and hence presumable financial interest therein. Miley said, however, that Miss Guinan appeared to be joking.

FROM "TEXAS FREE OF ONE CHARGE"
(*New York Times*, February 29, 1927)

Nuisance Case Dropped—Hostess Up for Contempt Tomorrow

The complaint charging that Texas Guinan had maintained a nuisance at the 300 Club in West Fifty-fourth Street, was dismissed yesterday by Federal Judge William Bondy without opposition from the United States Attorney's office.

Assistant United States Attorney Robert B. Watts, who opposed the motion to dismiss when it was argued some time ago, explained that the Government, having instituted contempt proceedings against Miss Guinan, did not wish to proceed on two charges against her, either of which would carry, upon conviction, imprisonment, or a fine, or both.

Hyman Edson and Jack Golden, employes of the 300 Club, who were also named in the nuisance charge, were freed of this complaint with Miss Guinan. Neither is involved in the contempt proceeding. Argument on the contempt motion will be made before Federal Judge Thomas D. Thacher tomorrow.

M. Michael Edelstein, attorney for Miss Guinan, said he would move for dismissal of the contempt charge on the ground that the temporary injunction which Miss Guinan is accused of having violated had been held illegal by Judge Thacher in his decision in test cases involving other defendants.

Mr. Edelstein said Miss Guinan was not the owner of the 300 Club, but had been employed there as hostess.

FROM "TEXAS GUINAN FREED ON LIQUOR CHARGE"
(*New York Times*, March 31, 1927)

The hearing before Federal Judge Thacher resulted yesterday in the acquittal of Texas Guinan, night club hostess, and Herman [*sic*] Edson, employe, who had been tried for contempt of court. It was disclosed that a bottle of alleged whiskey, seized from a bootlegger, had been taken from prohibition headquarters at 1 Park Avenue and used by a prohibition agent to aid him in establishing himself as a "good fellow" at the 300 Club, 151 West Fifty-fourth Street, where Miss Guinan was recently employed.

Truman Fowler, who said he was a student at New York University Law School, as well as one of the Prohibition Administrator Mills's agents, testified that he studied law in the daytime and sought information against prohibition law violators at night. He said the 300 Club had been his first assignment from Major Mills.

Fowler declared he had been unable on one visit to buy liquor at the 300 Club, but had purchased drinks there on subsequent visits. Fowler said he took a young woman to the club three times. Four other agents testified they had bought liquor in the club.

Judge Thacher, after hearing all the testimony, said the Government had failed to prove beyond a reasonable doubt that the defendants had participated in the sale of liquor on the premises. The alleged contempt consisted of having sold liquor in violation of a temporary injunction against the owners of the 300 Club.

"I certainly did not order any waiter to serve liquor to any patron at the 300 Club," Miss Guinan testified. "I think they sold liquor there at one time, but just before the holidays George Levy [Treasurer] gave orders that no more liquor was to be served."

According to Miss Guinan, Mr. Levy owned the club. She said she had signed a contract with him in December, 1925, to "put on the show" at the club for a weekly salary of $1,000, and "extras" for any additional shows. The club was raided and closed on Feb. 17 last.

Captain John W. Inglesby, Chief of the Padlock Division, testified he had served a preliminary injunction against the club on Dec. 22 last and had found the injunction in a cuspidor when he raided the place on Feb. 17. He said that when arrested at that time Miss Guinan had called to her brother "Tommy" Guinan and asked him to "bring along $500" as she "might want to play poker in the station house."

J. Walter Longcope, another college student and prohibition agent, testified he had seen Fowler buy whisky in the 300 club and had taken a drink of it. Other agents said that at a nod of the head from Miss Guinan the patron who asked for liquor received it. Agent Palmer Tubbs said a nod of Miss Guinan's head also caused waiters promptly to eject any person who had made himself objectionable.

Mr. Levy testified that no liquor had been sold in the club since Dec. 15, when he had given orders to every employe not to do so.

STUDY QUESTIONS

1. The accuracy of all the testimony you have just read is, at the least, open to question. Which of the testimonies you have read is most believable? Explain why.

2. What differences do you find between the New York *Herald Tribune* account of Rosenthal's murder and the *New York Times* account? Which are significant?

3. If you had only the newspaper accounts of Rosenthal's murder, how would you react to Police Commissioner Waldo's letter to District Attorney Whitman? Justify your answer.

4. If you had only the newspaper accounts, how trustworthy would you find Becker's statements about Rosenthal? Is there anything suspicious about them?

5. Do the newspaper accounts make Rosenthal look like a martyr? A hero? If you had only these accounts, what would be your opinion of Rosenthal?

6. What are the similarities between Rosenthal's murder and Rothstein's? What are the important differences?

7. How do you account for Mrs. Farry's testimony in the McManus trial? Was she angry? Had she been bribed? Was she telling the truth? Come to your own decision and then defend it.

8. What is the attitude of the *Times* reporter toward Mrs. Farry? Is it justified?

9. What is the attitude of the *Times* reporter toward the whole McManus trial and its outcome? What is your attitude? Remember that a man is being charged with murder.

10. Rothstein's murder remains unsolved. Why do you think this is so?

11. In what ways does Wolfsheim resemble Rothstein? Does Wolfsheim have qualities that it seems unlikely that Rothstein possessed? If so, what are they?

12. What impression of Comiskey do you get from the newspaper accounts?

13. If you had all the evidence available in this chapter (with the exception of Rothstein's papers found after his death), would you have indicted Rothstein? Defend your answer.

14. Doheny was eventually acquitted of bribery. How do you account for this? What in his testimony might make you think he was guilty?

15. Why do you think Fall was convicted although Doheny was acquitted?

16. Are the newspapers friendly toward Texas Guinan? Unfriendly? Explain.

17. Texas Guinan was almost a legend in the 1920s. What does this say about the spirit of the times? About the attitudes toward Prohibition?

18. If this were the 1920s and you had the money and the opportunity, would you patronize one of Guinan's clubs? Why or why not?

19. Write a description of Texas Guinan. Would you have liked to have known her? Explain.

20. Texas Guinan and the evangelist Aimee Semple McPherson admired each other and became friends. How do you account for this unlikely friendship?

21. How does Gatsby's murder differ from those you have read about in this chapter? Is the difference significant?

22. Does Gatsby share qualities with the gangsters mentioned above? Are there important differences?

TOPICS FOR WRITTEN OR ORAL EXPLORATION

1. Some novelists explicitly include material instead of alluding to it. A novelist like Theodore Dreiser, for example, might have included most of the factual material on Rosenthal in this chapter. Fitzgerald relies on quick allusion to it in the scene where Nick Carraway meets Wolfsheim. Would you prefer to read a version of *The Great Gatsby* containing all this information? Defend your answer.

2. One school of literary criticism holds that a work should be read entirely independent of background. Would you enjoy *The Great Gatsby* more if you had no background information? Justify your answer. First give your own preference, and then discuss what you think would be true of most readers.

3. Most readers in the 1920s had at least some knowledge of the events to which Fitzgerald alludes. Now fewer readers are familiar with them. Does this mean that the novel is dated? Defend your answer.

4. Organize a trial for Edward Doheny. If feasible, use additional evidence not included in this book. Let your jury decide guilt or innocence, and let your judge sentence the accused.

5. Try Texas Guinan in the same way.

6. The main problem with enforcing Prohibition was that many citizens thought the law was wrong and did not obey it. Can you think of similar examples from today? Dr. Jack Kevorkian, who helps termi-

nally ill people commit suicide, keeps getting acquitted by juries. If you were on a jury, would you convict him? Defend your answer.

7. If you had been on a jury, would you have convicted Texas Guinan? Defend your answer.

8. Today we have problems with illegal drug traffic and illegal drug use. In what ways is this similar to the situation during Prohibition? In what ways is it different?

9. Compare and contrast scandals in the Clinton administration with ones in the Harding administration. Is there a difference in public reaction? If so, what accounts for the difference?

10. Nick Carraway feels a great deal of sympathy for Gatsby. If Gatsby has been involved in the kinds of illegal activities described in this chapter, should anyone feel sorry for him? Do you? Justify your answer.

SUGGESTIONS FOR FURTHER READING

Adams, Samuel Hopkins. *Incredible Era: The Life and Times of Warren Gamaliel Harding*. Boston: Houghton Mifflin, 1939. Hopkins' book and Allen's *Only Yesterday* are the principal sources for information about Harding in this chapter.

Allen, Frederick Lewis. *Only Yesterday: An Informal History of the 1920's*. New York: Harper and Row, 1931. *Only Yesterday* is a general history of culture in the 1920s with excellent chapters on the Harding administration, on Prohibition, and on changing social behavior. The other books listed here focus on specific aspects of the period.

Asbury, Herbert. *The Great Illusion: An Informal History of Prohibition*. New York: Doubleday, 1950. This is a thorough history of the temperance movement in the United States and contains very colorful descriptions of New York life in the 1920s, including information about Larry Fay.

Bergreen, Laurence. *Capone: The Man and the Era*. New York: Simon and Schuster, 1994.

Berliner, Louise. *Texas Guinan: Queen of the Night Clubs*. Austin: University of Texas Press, 1993. This is an excellent full-length biography, especially valuable for its treatment of Guinan's nightclub career.

Clarke, Donald Henderson. *In the Reign of Rothstein*. New York: Grosset and Dunlap, 1929.

Epstein, Daniel Mark. *Sister Aimee: The Life of Aimee Semple McPherson*. New York: Harcourt Brace Jovanovich, 1993.

Gropman, Donald. *Say It Ain't So, Joe! The True Story of Shoeless Joe Jackson*. Rev. ed. New York: Carol, 1992.

Katcher, Leo. *The Big Bankroll: The Life and Times of Arnold Rothstein*. New York: Harper and Brothers, 1958.

Lewis, Alfred Allan. *Man of the World: Herbert Bayard Swope. A Charmed Life of Pulitzer Prizes, Poker and Politics*. Indianapolis: Bobbs-Merrill, 1978.

Noggle, Burl. *Teapot Dome: Oil and Politics in the 1920's*. Baton Rouge: Louisiana State University Press, 1962.

Shirley, Glenn. *"Hello, Sucker!" The Story of Texas Guinan*. Austin, TX: Eakin Press, 1989. This is a good introduction to the career of Texas Guinan.

Walker, Stanley. *The Nightclub Era*. New York: Frederick A. Stokes, 1933. Walker's book is a good supplement to Asbury's and contains additional information about Larry Fay.

4

The Woman Question: Changes during the 1920s

Fitzgerald's heroine, Daisy Buchanan, is a product of the 1920s. In 1900 it would have been highly unlikely for a woman of her social class to behave as freely and boldly as she does. Yet a woman today would be likely to find solutions to her love and marriage problems that Daisy does not. For example, for both social and economic reasons, divorce was then much less common than it is today. Daisy is in love with Gatsby and marries a very wealthy man when she feels Gatsby has abandoned her. She finds her life boring. Much worse than that, her husband is unfaithful and hardly bothers to hide it. She is passionately in love with Gatsby when he returns, but cannot bring herself to leave her husband, although she will not say that she never loved him.

Part of the explanation for her behavior lies in the position of women at the time. To understand that position, we need to look a moment at the women's movement in the early twentieth century. This movement had raised women's hopes by successfully lobbying for the passage of the Nineteenth Amendment to the Constitution, which was ratified in 1920, granting women the right to vote. Also, women's groups had been one of the major forces behind the movement to prohibit the sale of alcohol, and the Eighteenth Amendment to the Constitution, ratified in 1919, permitted Congress to make Prohibition an established fact.

Margaret Sanger was distributing birth control information in a way that would have been impossible earlier. It is true that she was both prosecuted and persecuted and that organizations such as Anthony Comstock's New York Society for the Prevention of Vice still seriously preached that the only way to keep women virtuous was to keep them sexually ignorant. It is true that Comstock's organization prosecuted many who attempted to provide birth control information or sex education. Yet, in spite of all this opposition, birth control information was being spread.

Women were now demanding more than they were before. A few years before, upper-class and middle-class women were expected to be obedient to husbands and to devote most of their energy to being mothers. Many of them had accepted the double standard and looked the other way when husbands were unfaithful.

But the new generation of women wanted much more from marriage and from life. They wanted to be partners with their husbands. They wanted romance and good sex lives. They wanted independence. The result of these desires was a social revolution.

Young women now smoked cigarettes, wore makeup, and danced all night. They discussed sex openly. Unmarried women flirted, necked, and petted, and at times even had sex. They engaged in sports like tennis, golf, and swimming. Fashions reflected the new liberation. Skirts became looser, providing greater leg freedom, and in the course of the 1920s hemlines rose from the ankles to the knee. Daring women removed their corsets for dancing and rolled their stockings beneath the knees visible under their short skirts. These young women were the flappers who became the subject of much of Fitzgerald's fiction.

Yet there was a catch to all this freedom: there was little political foundation for it and almost no economic foundation. In the 1920s women's suffrage did not bring women political power. Politicians gradually realized that women were not voting as a bloc on issues that concerned them. For a few years politicians experimented with courting women's votes, sometimes in very clumsy and amusing ways. In 1920, for example, the Republican party ran a full-page advertisement in the *American Magazine* featuring pictures of the mothers of the presidential and vice-presidential candidates. But by the end of the 1920s the major parties were ignoring women's needs. Economically, women were only a little better off than they had been earlier. They made headway in a few professions, but it was still very difficult for most women to be economically independent.

For women generally, marriage was the only real career available. Economic necessity had a great deal to do with whether a woman married and which man she married. Women from lower economic classes might be expected to work at low-paying jobs both before and after marriage; most of these jobs did not pay enough to allow women to live an independent life. Women from middle and upper classes had very few job opportunities that led to genuine careers. But even more important than the lack of opportunity was the general assumption that a woman's only real career was marriage. Her social and economic status was provided by her husband.

Sarah Beebe Fryer's *Fitzgerald's New Women: Harbingers of Change* offers an excellent description of the economic plight of Fitzgerald's heroines. Earlier critics, such as Leslie Fiedler in *Love and Death in the American Novel*, to take an extreme example, describe Fitzgerald's heroines as attractive, destructive leeches, but Fryer points out that Fitzgerald realizes, either consciously or unconsciously, the pressures these women felt. The fact remains, however, that most critics have agreed that Fitzgerald often feels hostility toward the women he creates, and in his personal life he exhibited a great deal of hostility toward his wife, Zelda. It is up to you, as a reader of *The Great Gatsby*, to decide whether the view of Fryer or the view of Fiedler is closer to the truth in this particular novel.

Daisy's economic position is very important to this novel, and Gatsby's worship of Daisy is closely tied to his attitude toward money. Fitzgerald, in his personal life, was very aware of the importance of money. Remember that Gatsby once says that Daisy's voice is "full of money." Yet it would be a mistake to say that the novel is about money and nothing else, or that what it says about money is all that simple. Gatsby is attracted to Daisy because she is rich, but at the same time he has no designs on her wealth. He will not try to win her again until he has wealth of his own.

It is important to remember that Daisy is a sort of financial prisoner. Her lifestyle depends on Tom's money. She has no real way of making money on her own. Gatsby has money, but his wealth, like his whole future, is precarious. But here again the issue is not simple. A woman might marry for money and status, but might it also be true that money and status make the man himself attractive? Fitzgerald once said that money and "great animal magnetism" were the most important things in attracting women. He also said that the next most important things were good looks and intelligence and that he got the "top girl" by using those. There is a very strong bond between Tom and Daisy. It is up to you to decide what it is.

The documents in this chapter examine three important aspects of women's social and economic position in the 1920s. The first shows the reaction to what was then a new phenomenon—an outstanding woman athlete. The second document is a profile of a strikingly successful woman executive—an unusual phenomenon in the 1920s. The final document looks at social qualities of adolescent girls in the 1920s as seen through the eyes of G. Stanley Hall, a brilliant, widely experienced scholar, psychological therapist, and educator in his late seventies who is trying to understand new patterns of behavior. Notice what these articles tell you about the world of Jordan Baker, Myrtle Wilson, and Daisy Buchanan.

GERTRUDE EDERLE

Gertrude Ederle was treated as an international heroine in 1926 when she not only became the first woman to swim the English Channel, but also swam it faster than any of the five men who swam it before her. Today we take it for granted that women excel in sports. This was not the case in the 1920s.

It was at this time that women began to win prizes in golf, tennis, and swimming, and in some cases they competed successfully against men. In the late nineteenth century many authorities had considered women too delicate for strenuous exercise. It was even seriously suggested that women should eat only bland, soft foods and avoid things like meat, which put too much strain on their digestive systems. Even in the nineteenth century, though, not everyone held such extreme views. The heroine of Louisa May Alcott's *Eight Cousins*, for example, is taught to live healthfully. Still, it was not until the 1920s that women athletes began to come into their own.

As you read the following article, bear in mind how stupendous Gertrude Ederle's achievement was. Imagine yourself swimming thirty-one miles in fourteen hours and thirty-one minutes by doing laps in an ordinary pool. Now imagine doing it in cold water, with frequent rain and heavy winds, with waves so strong that they often throw the swimmer back great distances. While Gertrude Ederle was swimming the Channel, the weather was so bad that the captain of the boat thought for a time that he could not land at Dover. Her coach repeatedly told her to give up and come out of the water. Strength, endurance, great skill, and extraordinary will-power—Gertrude Ederle had all of these things.

The title contains a reference to a classical legend. Leander was a young man who lived in Abydos, a city on the Asian side of the Dardanelles or Hellespont, a narrow body of water between Asia Minor and the European mainland. He fell in love with Hero, a priestess of Aphrodite who lived in Sestos, a city on the European side. According to the legend, he swam the Hellespont to see her. Finally he drowned in a storm, and his body was washed up on Hero's side. When she learned that he was dead, she drowned herself.

Gertrude Ederle at the time of her victory.

is a creek compared with the English Channel. He swam for love, she for glory, and those two motives are equally sacred to the poets. No hero of all antiquity was more worthy of laurels than the German-American butcher's daughter, and none ever received anything approaching the multitudinous homage that is now being paid to her. Not a dissentient note could mar it. There may be grumblings at the adulation showered on a Red Grange or even a Babe Ruth, but no heart grudges a single cheer of the chorus flung at Gertrude Ederle. Her victory is so clean and so brave, so complete and so overwhelming!

The article continues with accounts from several newspapers that raise interesting points about public opinion. "Uncle Dudley" writes in the Boston *Daily Globe*: "And now the channel has been the means of giving women new dignity. . . . Very reluctantly the males, the lords of creation, admit that the females of the species are anything better than second raters." The Jersey *Journal*, after commenting that gamblers were betting three to one against Gertrude Ederle, notes: "Well, women got the vote; their votes helped put prohibition over. They won lots of other things, and now they hold the greatest of swimming records. . . . The feminists are surely having their innings despite 'Ma' Ferguson's defeat." "Ma" (Miriam A. Wallace) Ferguson had just lost the primary in her campaign for reelection as governor of Texas, an office she had won in 1924. The real authority in her administration belonged to her husband, "Pa" (James Edward) Ferguson, who was barred from seeking the office himself after he was impeached in 1917 while serving as governor. The Syracuse *Herald* quotes Tom Robison, who taught swimming at Northwestern University, as saying that thirty years earlier women could not have done what Gertrude Ederle had done, "for corsets and other ridiculously unnecessary clothing hampered her physical condition and deprived her of the muscular effort so necessary in the development of a good swimmer. Physical education has wrought a complete turnover, not only in woman's physical condition but in her whole mental attitude." The Washington *Star* says: "Much benefit to American womanhood will result from the world-wide fame earned by Gertrude Ederle. The development of physical grace, strength and health will be most useful to the race."

Alec Rutherford, who cabled a firsthand account to the *New York Times*, describes how Gertrude Ederle continued to swim in cold

At its narrowest point the Hellespont is about a mile across,
short distance compared to the width of the English Channel. Still
people consider it a challenge to take Leander's swim. Maybe this
is partly because they like the idea of swimming from one conti
nent to another. The poet Byron is one of the most famous of
those who tried it successfully.

FROM "HOW A GIRL BEAT LEANDER AT THE HERO GAME"
(Literary Digest, August 21, 1926, pp. 52–67)

"ALL THE WOMEN OF THE WORLD will celebrate, too," prophesied "the
bob-haired, nineteen-year-old daughter of the Jazz Age," in forecasting
her victory to a New York sports editor. It was spoken lightly, "a little
shyly," but with evident realization that her triumph over the choppy,
chilly, changeable, treacherous, tide-driven, squally, fog-haunted English
Channel, supreme challenge of aquatic heroes and baffler of supermen,
would be hailed as a battle won for feminism. And in making that prediction as recorded by Mr. W. O. McGeehan in *The Herald Tribune*, Miss
Ederle probably had no premonition that she would beat the time of the
few male swimmers who had managed to perform the Herculean task of
forging their way between England and France. With that added feather
in her cap—the setting of a time record that possibly may never be
equaled by a man—she stands today as Champion Extraordinary of her
sex, and its unanswerable refutation of the masculinist dogma that
woman is, in the sense of physical power and efficiency, inferior to man.
Nay, her great achievement may bring it to be acknowledged that Mr.
Kipling knew what he was talking about when he proclaimed lyrically,
"The female of the species is more deadly than the male"; and it needs
no fantastic stretch of the imagination to picture the Channel swimming
of the future as having its liveliest interest centered in the gallant and
somewhat pathetic efforts of masculine swimmers to equal the feminine
record! Apropos of which one could almost spare a tear for the dignified
London newspaper which, on the very day of "Trudie's" destined triumph, put in type for the following day a calm and scholarly editorial
commenting on the futility of competitive athletics for women, on the
ground that they must ever remain athletically inferior to men—the sad-
dest part of the story being, according to London correspondents, that
the news of the New York girl's triumph came too late for the dismayed
editors to "kill" that singularly untimely preachment. And now, with all
the world throwing flowers at her feet, Miss Ederle may reflect that Ho-
mer would have hymned her victory had it occurred in the days of early
Greece, and she would have become a heroine of myth and drama. Leander's laurels would have been lowered many points, for the Hellespont

water and stormy weather until someone finally said, "Gertie, you must come out!" She replied, "What for?" The *Daily News* quotes Gertrude Ederle as saying: "I never once felt tired during the swim. The thought of giving up never entered my mind. I never could have swum the channel tho if I hadn't had the encouragement of my pals aboard the accompanying *Alsace*."

The *Herald Tribune* quotes suffragist Carrie Chapman Catt as saying, "We are very proud of Miss Ederle, proud that a woman swimmer and an American has at last made a record swim in the English Channel." After discussing the importance of woman's strength and health in the struggle for equality, Catt adds, "The American woman is a far better specimen than she was two generations ago, and she is ashamed to be ill."

This cross section of comments gives some notion of the impact made by Gertrude Ederle. First and very clearly, there is the drama of the struggle and the elation of winning. But in some cases there is an obvious uneasiness behind the humor and slight condescension. Some express genuine awestruck admiration, others an almost clinical recognition that the female human body has been freed from artificial limitations and has now come into its own. From Catt comes a recognition of the social implications of the new physical achievements of women. Gertrude Ederle, like the girls of Fitzgerald's fiction and like many real life women and girls of the 1920s, was unsettling. The world was changing drastically.

MARY DILLON

Mary Dillon was at forty-three the president of the Brooklyn Borough Gas Company and respected throughout her profession as an intelligent, knowledgeable leader. The following article about her career, published in the *American Magazine* in 1929, is an example of the kind of success story Americans of the 1920s loved to read. This was an age addicted to hero worship. People looked for heroes in every field and idolized entertainment and sports figures. But to many Americans the greatest heroes were those who succeeded in business.

Readers loved to learn how someone from an ordinary background had become wealthy or risen in the world through hard work, cleverness, patience, and the willingness to endure hardships and setbacks. But except for a few owners of small businesses, the subjects of these stories were nearly all men. Women worked, of course, as nurses, teachers, and secretaries, and in many jobs with low pay and low prestige. They made inroads as medical doctors and in higher education, especially in the social sciences. But it was still very difficult for a woman to become a major business executive. It happened so seldom that those who succeeded in this field seemed to be freaks.

Some of the attitudes about women's place in the business world expressed by Dillon as well as by the author may seem strange to a modern reader. Some of them may make you angry or make you laugh—or both. But bear in mind that these attitudes would have been the conscious or unconscious assumptions of Fitzgerald's characters and for the most part those of Fitzgerald himself.

FROM HELEN CHRISTINE BENNETT, *"DOES* BUSINESS *GIVE* WOMEN A SQUARE DEAL?"
(*American Magazine*, February 1929, pp. 40, 96, 97, 102, 104)

It does, says MARY DILLON, *except that a woman to reach the top must work much harder than a man*.

The Sixth Annual Convention of the American Gas Association was in

progress. In the hall were assembled the officers and managers of practically all the gas supply companies of the country. As the chairman announced the new speaker, there was a rustle, a sudden stiffening of backs
and raising of eyes.

"First time a woman ever spoke on this platform," said the general
manager of one of the biggest companies to the official who sat next to
him.

"She's been coming here for years, though," replied his companion.
"Ought not to mind us."

He stopped to listen. The small, trim-tailored, very feminine figure
upon the platform was apparently not "minding" them. She stood easily,
naturally, while her well-modulated, resonant tones filled the room. But
despite her outward composure, within her lurked an anxiety born of
great responsibility. Upon this platform Mary E. Dillon was making history. No woman had before occupied the position of general manager of
a gas company, no woman had ever spoken at this convention. The
twenty-one years of service to her company had made her a "good gasman."

How could she demonstrate that women belonged in this broader
field?

She spoke briefly, in pithy sentences, for she was talking upon the
newest and most urgent problem of the gas industry, the exact relation
of a public utility company to its consuming public. And she spoke from
the standpoint of what she herself had done. When she had concluded
and the warm round of applause had subsided, the first man turned to
his companion.

"That girl knows more than gas; she knows people," he said. "Bet you
they make her president some day."

"A woman-president!" exclaimed the other. "Not in our day."

It was exactly two years later that the first speaker's prophecy came
true.

In the field of public relationship Mary Dillon is recognized as a leader.
Her interpretation of the place of a gas company in the lives of the citizens it serves is unique and far-reaching. It has also been successful in
the practical administration of the affairs of the Brooklyn Borough Gas
Company. The name of the Company may be a bit misleading. Its headquarters are at Coney Island [Coney Island is best known as the location
of an enormous amusement park]. From the incubator babies on the
Boardwalk and the Bowery, kept warm by gas heat, to the smoke of the
sham Battle of Château Thierry, the great amusement centers of the famous resort present unusual service problems. But the bulk of the work
is in furnishing gas to homes and industries and it is in this routine
service of a public utility that Miss Dillon has made her record.

On my first trip to see her, I walked past the building which houses the offices of the Company, and then past again. I was looking for a gas company's building. The building I had passed and repassed bore no resemblance to the usual structure given over to such a purpose. Finally, convinced by a not too conspicuous sign that this *was* the building, I stopped on the pavement and gave it a thorough looking over before entering. If you are growing a bit impatient and want to get to Mary Dillon, be satisfied. For this building is Mary Dillon. It was planned by her when she was a general manager, it's every detail is hers, and its unique character is indicative of her distinctive belief and methods in the conduct of her business. This low, red-brick building, colonial in feeling, with its balconied window boxes filled with flowering plants leaning over from the second floor, is a beautiful, friendly contribution to the appearance of the street.

As I entered, I again stopped to observe. Apparently almost the whole first floor is in one large, tile-floored hall, which rises to a height of three stories. Near the top are many-paned large windows, with green shutters decorated with a cut out, lighted torch. Below these windows, more balconied boxes filled with flowers. On the floor about me stood the display of an up-to-date gas company, immaculate stoves, refrigerators, irons, heaters, and halfway down one side rose a curved white marble staircase, with a landing upon which real ivy grew up a trellis to a balcony. Off that balcony lies the president's office. By the time I arrived there I was prepared for the wicker furniture, the Martha Washington sewing table, the shelves of books. Among these stood the usual executive desk. From behind it stepped a small figure, five feet exactly, attired in a smart tailored dress, and a hand found mine, while a pleasant contralto voice bade me welcome.

Mary Dillon's whole appearance is unassertive, but there is strength in the unusual forehead, very wide at its top, in the straight nose, in the mobile and beautiful mouth. She has two big dimples and these transform her face into that of a laughter-loving girl.

As we lunched upon simple, well-cooked food that is served every day to the employees of the Company, she spoke, with the dimples again in evidence, of the difficulties of a gasman of Coney Island.

"When I am traveling," she said, laughing, "and tell folks that I'm from Coney Island, I am prepared for a startled and delighted expression on their faces. When it becomes evident that I am not a human centipede, or that my hair cannot rival the golden locks of a Circassian beauty, I can see them relegate me to a lower plane, but still hopefully. For I may be a fortune teller, a trapeze performer, a dancer or snake charmer, or Katie the human fly! I never can quite bear the disappointment manifested when I confess I am a gasman, a respectable calling but gray as the sands of the sea on a rainy day."

Gray? Well, you shall be the judge. For to me there is a rosy glow about Mary Dillon from the time twenty-five years ago, when she decided to become an errand boy, until today. She is not merely a pioneer in a business new to a woman. As an executive she has also won the admiration and respect of the men in the gas industry. Since she has dictated its policies, her company has been marked as signally successful. Its growth has been rapid—so rapid indeed that problems of finance and construction have been a regular part of the year's program. Its dividends are paid regularly and there is a surplus.

As a part of her work as president, Mary E. Dillon has made herself a vital part of her community. She is a director of the Brooklyn Chamber of Commerce, and a director of the Coney Island Chamber of Commerce; secretary and director of the Coney Island Hotel Corporation, which operates the community-owned Half Moon Hotel at Coney Island. She is an officer and director of the Coney Island Center and of the Carnival Company of Coney Island, and the chairman of the Finance Committee of the Harbor Hospital, Brooklyn. And she is a consultant to hundreds of people on any problem affecting community interests.

What has this to do with a gas company? Mary Dillon would tell you that it is essential to its successful administration. Adopting as a business policy the theory that her services belong to the community, she has grown into one of those rare human beings who are always consulted when anything of importance to their neighbors is to happen.

She was one of twelve children born to Philip and Ann Eliza Dillon. Her father was an employee of the United States Post Office, and his salary of eighteen hundred dollars a year—which of course had a buying power of almost twice that amount today—was carefully and cleverly budgeted, so that the family lived nicely upon the sum. It was a home like thousands of American homes, where father and mother and children lived happy, golden days of struggle, glorified by their mutual love.

"An old-fashioned Christian home," said Miss Dillon.

From this old-fashioned home have grown to maturity eight useful men and women. Henry Dillon, one of Mary's older brothers, entered the Gas Company a year after Mary, and is today its general superintendent and a director.

In her senior year at high school Mary decided to work through the summer vacation. Coney Island presented opportunities, and she got a job at Louis Stauch's bathhouses. Her duties were simple. She stood at the bathingsuit counter, surveyed the feminine applicants for bathing suits, decided whether the woman before her wore a thirty-six or a forty-two, and passed out the correct size. Her success at the job depended upon the accuracy of her appraisal, because if the suit did not fit, returns made a lot of trouble. Mary did very well and she suspected that the six dollars a week she was receiving was not all to which she was entitled. She investigated. Her partner, who was doing exactly the same work, was receiving seven dollars a week. Mary sought Mr. Stauch, presented her facts, and asked for a raise of a dollar a week.

"I am doing the same work," she argued, "and doing it just as well." Mr. Stauch shook his head. Mary was new, she might not last. He refused. Today, as a retired magnate, Stauch tells the story and laughs heartily.

"The one mistake of my business career," he says, twinkling, "was when I turned down Mary Dillon."

Refused her raise, Mary took action. Her sister Eva was employed by the Gas Company, but was to leave to be married. Mary decided to try for her place. She asked Eva to see the superintendent James J. Humphrey.

"H'm, is your sister the girl who won that prize given by the 'New York Times' for the best essay on Hendrik Hudson and the Half Moon?" asked Humphrey.

"Yes, she is," said Eva Dillon.

"Send her along," said the superintendent. So Mary, on the strength of a prize essay, entered the Brooklyn Borough Gas Company as a kind of general utility clerk, or office-boy. She had decided not to go back to school; she wanted to work.

It was gray work, if you saw it that way. For she began by filling inkwells and sharpening pencils and running errands from office to office. But it was a small company at that time. Mary found an opportunity to fit in many capacities. For three happy, eager years she burrowed into the affairs of the Gas Company, ferreting out information, her sharp eyes seeing, and her mathematical mind classifying, and her scientific faculty relating what she saw and heard. She became a very mine of information even at that early day.

At the end of her third year with the Company, there was need for a new office manager. James J. Humphrey, the general manager, wanted Mary Dillon to be his office manager; she possessed both the ability and the knowledge to handle the job well. But Mary Dillon was a charming young woman with the joy of life abounding within her. No such office manager had ever been known in a gas company office. The only other available employee was John H. Bailey. Mr. Humphrey debated the matter and decided upon Mr. Bailey as his next office manager. He sent for Bailey and spoke frankly.

"I've been hesitating," he said, "between you and Miss Dillon. But I don't want a woman as office manager, and so I am giving the job to you."

Then John H. Bailey, with the job in his hand, spoke.

"Mr. Humphrey," he said, "give Miss Dillon this job. It doesn't matter about her being a woman. She can fill the place better than I can. Give it to her."

After a long conference, Bailey went out. Humphrey sent for Mary Dillon.

"She was just twenty-one, and although I dislike applying to a woman of Mary Dillon's ability the adjective 'pretty,' there is no doubt that she merited it at twenty-one (and still does today at forty-three)." Humphrey looked at the girl before him, at her curly hair with its glints of gold, her bright blue eyes and her lovely mouth, and he sighed. She didn't look like an office manager; she looked like a girl any young man might capture at any time—without notice. He said something to this effect.

"All right, then," said Mary Dillon. "I'll give you my word I won't marry."

And thus, upon a pledge of spinsterhood and with John Bailey withdrawing in her favor, Mary Dillon became office manager.

John Bailey is now manager of distribution for the Brooklyn Borough Gas Company and a warm friend of its president. When, as president, Miss Dillon presented Bailey with the medal given by the Company at the end of twenty-five years of service, she told this story.

"You did not know that I knew," she said to Bailey, "but after a time Mr. Humphrey told me. One never knows what might have happened, but I owe you my job. You are a good sportsman!"

Under the title of office manager Mary Dillon served the Brooklyn Borough Gas Company for thirteen years. Her first promotions had been rapid; her growth following was with that of the Company. Mr. Humphrey resigned and was succeeded by Mr. G. H. Woodall. To these two men Mary E. Dillon credits much of her training. Humphrey, the technician, the engineer, the conservative, and Woodall, a liberal, an administrator with a distinct flair for public relationship, guided the young woman in just that combination of qualities essential for an able executive. Both men were generous with their help.

"But that," she assured me, "is true of most of the men I have met in business."

In 1916–1917 the eighty-cent gas rate was ordered by legislative action for New York. The Brooklyn Borough Gas Company could not do business on an eighty-cent rate. It served a widespread territory. In one section the mains ran for miles without being tapped for service. The Company appealed for a rate decision giving it the right to charge more for gas. The attorney for the Gas Company decided that Miss Dillon knew more about the matter than anyone else and that she should be chief witness for the Company.

When Mary Dillon heard that decision, she had for days the awful sensation of fear that almost paralyzes one's tongue and one's brain. But she never thought of side-stepping or protesting. Long before, she had evolved a guiding principle that she applied to her job as officer manager and to herself as a human being:

"Accept as a gift from Heaven the opportunity to try new work."

The exact relation of the trying of a rate case to a gift from Heaven did not disturb her as she sat day after day at the long, mahogany table in the office of Charles Evans Hughes, the referee, and replied to the questions asked her, questions that required every bit of the knowledge she had been accumulating all the sixteen years she had been a gasman. Technical details upon the manufacture of gas, operating expense, cost of laying mains and pipes, distribution area, pressure, topography of the territory served, office expense, peak loads—these formed the basis for question after question which she met and answered readily, calmly, and succinctly.

Before the hearings had ended Mary Dillon was accepted as a sensation. Reporters from newspapers spread her fame far and wide, the attorneys became friendly, those in attendance begged to meet her, and within herself her heart sang. She knew that she had established herself as a gasman.

When her testimony was concluded the city counsel turned to the attorneys present.

"Gentlemen," he said, "if all our witnesses were as well-informed and as honest and fair as this young woman, we would get to the marrow of these rate cases in no time."

When the decision was handed down by Charles E. Hughes, the Brooklyn Borough Gas Company had won its appeal, thanks largely to Mary Dillon.

Two years later the general manager of the Company left. Miss Dillon was the obvious person for the vacant place. But the owners of the Company demurred. A woman as an office manager might be possible; as a general manager, it was beyond anything heard of in a gas company. Yet they needed Mary Dillon. For five years she worked on, and the general managership remained an empty title. In fact, she was the general manager, but without recognition.

In 1924, after the five years of service without a title, the Board of Directors made Miss Dillon general manager and vice president. A year later, the controlling interest of the Company was sold and when the new president, Mr. Frank Hulswit, came into office he at once recognized how much the Company owed to Mary Dillon.

Something of the general change in the attitude towards women in industry was reflected in this belated granting of office; for shortly before it had come Miss Dillon had married. And her pledge to spinsterhood was long outdated. No one in the Company now objected; no one expected her to resign. But there was considerable curiosity as to the man she had chosen as her husband.

Henry Farber stood inspection well. The curious found him a man who had made a considerable personal success, who was now interested in the coal business, and who bore with perfect equanimity and even a suspicion of pride the fact that his wife was a distinguished personality in the gas industry.

"How did you ever live through those years when you did all the work without the title?" I asked her.

"I had not demonstrated my ability sufficiently," she replied, "and I had to remember day after day that no woman had ever occupied such a position, that my fitness for it would have to be shown again and again. It was entirely a question of sex: all precedent, all custom was against me. I was willing to give those five years, or any number of required years, until my demonstration was effective."

There is behind that statement a belief in herself that is sustaining. Mary Dillon's faith has always held her to her work.

To understand her work it is necessary to know something of Coney Island. If you had not seen that great playground for many years and you were taken there via airplane and dropped on the wide boardwalk running along the edge of the ocean, you would never recognize the Coney Island of fifteen years ago. The fifty millions of people who go there each summer must rejoice in this new, clean, and spick-and-span walk, with its shops and bathhouses, its restaurants and amusements. Behind it lives a little of the old Coney Island, but it is neater and cleaner and smarter. No matter how many thousands of bathers leave their papers upon the sands, the next morning the beach is clean, the walks immaculate. In all of this Mary Dillon's feminine fingers have had a large part. The gas company building is a part of the new plan, not only of exquisite neatness, but of personal service, for Miss Dillon makes a special point of having her customers well treated. Any one of them can see her for the asking. And often they do ask. Not long ago a man who had just moved to the Island brought his wife with him to ask that his home be supplied with gas.

"My child is seek," he said, waving his arms wildly; "we musta have the gas . . . and queek! queek!" Then he turned to his wife and ordered, "Now you cry! Cry, do you hear, Cry!"

Miss Dillon managed to stop the demonstration by promising gas at once, and the pair went away, talking of "nice presents" if the gas went on. "Nice presents" to the office are many. They have included a quantity of fresh liver wrapped in a newspaper, bags of rolls, candy, and on one occasion the treasurer of the company was awarded a dime. In order to avoid hurting customer's feelings, these small gifts were accepted.

All Coney Island knows the gas company building, not only as a gas building but as a general meeting-place. If there is need for a clearing house for a general discussion, the gas offices are mutual ground.

If anyone asks Miss Dillon how a utility company can do this and if the cost is not considerable, she points out that the cost is merely a little extra janitor and porter service and that the Company profits in good will. When she spoke to the American Gas Association in 1924 she said:

"This business of ours has such varied and absorbing problems of engineering, accounting, and finance that in their solution we are likely to lose sight of the fact that they constitute just one half of the show. *These* matters are handled with the highest degree of efficiency, and they should be, for they have had the almost undivided attention of the cream of the gas industry for many years. I firmly believe that if the gas industry were to develop and follow a technique in dealing with its public comparable in excellence with that which it now employs in the manufacture and distribution of its products, the politicians would find other texts to serve their purposes, and our lawyers could take a rest at their own expense."

"We all try to do what Miss Dillon is doing," said an officer of one of the biggest gas companies.

As a pioneer in an industry which at her entry was practically closed to women, she has felt keenly the responsibility to her sex. In her company, there is no discrimination against women as such: offices depend entirely upon efficiency. In fact, they are rather evenly divided between men and women. At present the vice president is a man, the secretary and treasurer are women, the general superintendent is a man. But even in the manufacturing end of the business, Mary Dillon sees no bar to women workers. She herself is familiar with the gas plant; it was she who insisted that it should be as neat and attractive as possible. Its light-yellow painted walls and clear floors and its meticulous order are of her planning. This year a garden lies at its base.

"Business is in many cases dreary and drab," she said. "It needs all the color women can bring to it. All the social grace they have acquired in the administration of their homes is wanted there."

Her views on women employees are novel and refreshing.

"I prefer married women," she says, "because they are more stable, more fully matured and usually more in earnest. No woman loses her job here because she marries. And if she wishes to have a baby she can obtain a leave of absence for that purpose and later return to her place. In no case has their value altered except for the better."

For a year and a half I have been in touch with Miss Dillon with this article in mind. In that time I have just begun to get acquainted with the real woman. Affable, pleasant, interested in you and your mission, and with a warmth in her friendliness, she still conveys an impression that within herself she is living more deeply and more fully in the vision of the future than in either present or past. It was hard for Mary Dillon to talk of her childhood and girlhood, and she had had great difficulty in recalling as many of the details as I have given here.

"I don't do it at all well," she said. "I am sorry. I think—" she hesitated, "it is because I am too young. I am forty-three," she added, smiling as if to correct any misapprehension upon my part. "Perhaps that is not really young, but things that are past do not interest me particularly. I may enjoy looking back when I am—say, sixty-three. Now I keep my eyes on the present and the future. Tremendous changes are taking place in the industrial structure of the world, and the builders are men of during, of prophetic vision. How they will deal with the problems that are coming—not those of property but those that concern the human element— is and will be of the most vital interest to me."

G. STANLEY HALL ON THE FLAPPER

F. Scott Fitzgerald learned about flappers from life. The following article describes the flapper as a social phenomenon from the point of view of a scholarly observer. The author, G. Stanley Hall, was a very successful psychologist much concerned with women and motherhood. He was a major figure in the National Conference of Mothers, which eventually became the Parent-Teacher Association, as well as one of the founders of the American Psychological Association. He taught at the most prominent universities in the United States and was considered an authority on adolescent development. A student of William James at Harvard, Hall later taught John Dewey, perhaps the single most influential person in the history of modern American education. Born in 1844, Hall was in his late seventies when he wrote this article. A sophisticated man with clinical experience, he was familiar with the work of Darwin and Freud. Now, at the end of a long, distinguished career, he was trying to understand something in his line of work that was very new to him.

Hall's tone and style are conservative, even for established, cultured magazines of the time. The article is a good source on details of the flapper's tastes and habits, and it correctly observes that the flapper, like her mother, looked forward to marriage and a family. But does it ignore or gloss over much that did not seem "the same" or "all right"? In answering that question, bear in mind that cultivated writers of Hall's generation were not inclined to make shocking or vulgar statements directly. They relied on hints they expected intelligent readers to catch.

Fitzgerald, by contrast, makes his heroines behave in ways then considered shocking. Amory Blaine in *This Side of Paradise* finds that girls all over the country are kissing boys who are nearly strangers. At a time when girls were supposed to be engaged before they kissed, Amory's girlfriend Rosalind Connage says, "I've kissed dozens of men. I suppose I'll kiss dozens more." These flappers leave behind them whole strings of ex-boyfriends of whom they have tired. Like Rosalind Connage, they are often athletic. Rosalind embarrasses a boy by making a dangerous dive in front of him, leaving him no choice but to follow suit. Generally Fitzgerald's heroines are destructive, leaving broken-hearted men and confused lives behind them.

The assertive males in Fitzgerald's fiction hope to become financially successful. The flappers, as both Hall and Fitzgerald describe them, do not think of themselves as possible financial successes. Hall sees them as a new variety of potential mothers. To Fitzgerald the flappers are many things. They are glamorous. They are love objects. They are pleasure objects. They inspire men to seek success, but the inspiration they provide often turns out to be a delusion. However, the flapper does not seek economic success in her own right. For all her new freedom, she is without visible means of support until a male agrees to support her.

Note the difference between G. Stanley Hall's world view and Fitzgerald's simply by contrasting the way they write. Compare Hall's style with the style of *The Great Gatsby*. Hall is writing for the *Atlantic Monthly*, a conservative, highly respected magazine, in a style that was already old-fashioned in 1922. He relies heavily on words of Greek and Latin origin and on phrases borrowed from other languages, often using them half playfully. The style is meant to be dignified and mildly humorous. To a modern reader it is likely to seem bland and stuffy. Remember that Hall's flappers are somewhat younger than Fitzgerald's. Hall mentions the age of 17, and when he discusses high school girls, one can assume that most of the girls are 17 or younger. Yet the differences between Hall's view of the flappers and Fitzgerald's cannot be explained simply as a difference in the ages of the girls they describe. Some of Fitzgerald's early heroines are no more than 18. Zelda Sayre, the model for Rosalind Connage, was barely 18 when Fitzgerald met her, and was already behaving like the flappers in his fiction.

FROM G. STANLEY HALL, "FLAPPER AMERICANA NOVISSIMA"[1]
(*Atlantic Monthly*, June 1922, pp. 771–80)

I

When, years ago, I first heard the picturesque word "Flapper" applied to a girl, I thought of a loose sail flapping in whatever wind may blow, and liable to upset the craft it is meant to impel. There was also in my mind the flitting and yet cruder mental imagery of a wash, just hung out to dry in the light and breeze, before it is starched and ironed for use. I was a little ashamed of this when the dictionary set me right by defining the word as a fledgling, yet in the nest, and vainly attempting to fly while its wings have only pinfeathers; and I recognized that thus the genius of "slanguage" had made the squab the symbol of budding girlhood. This, too, had the advantage of a moral, implying what would happen if the young bird really ventured to trust itself to its pinions prematurely.

The Germans were a century ahead of us in naming this fascinating stage of human life; but their designation of it is most unpoetic, not to say culinary. To them the flapper is a fish all prepared for baking, but not yet subjected to that process. Indeed, *b* and *k* are so much alike that I cannot but wonder if the dull Teutonic lexicographers have not mistaken *Backfisch* for *Bachfisch*.[2] If so, she was meant to be named in that country from those piscene [*sic*] forms which, having been hatched far inland near the source of great rivers, have migrated, or been carried downstream, as they grew, and are found disporting in a broad estuary and adapting themselves to the boundless sea where they are henceforth to live. Perhaps the German who first applied this epithet did not mean to be so much unromantic and ungallant to the sex as fundamental; for all know that fish not only long preceded birds, in the order of evolution, but were their direct progenitors. On this line of conjecture the French *tendron* is still more fundamental, for it goes back to the vegetable kingdom, and dubs girls shoots, scions ready for grafting, buds, or perhaps organs yet undifferentiated and in the gristle stage. Had girls been themselves consulted, they might have hesitated between bird and bud, but surely never would have accepted fish. The angler at the other end of the tackle might possibly have been considered.

We must, then, admit at the outset that the world has not yet found the right designation for this unique product of civilization, the girl in the early teens, who is just now undergoing such a marvelous development. But why bother about names?

As a lifelong student of human nature, I long ago realized that of all the stages of human life this was *terra incognita*.[3] We now know much of children, of adults, and of old age, while the pubescent boy has become an open book. So I began months ago to forage in libraries, and was surprised to find how sentimental, imaginative, and altogether unscientific most of the few books, and the scores of articles, about girls in the early teens really were. Very persistent is the tendency to treat this grave and serious theme flippantly—to invoke Puck, Ariel, or Momus as the only muses who can help us in threading the labyrinthine mazes of feminine pubescence. Moreover, since the war, the kind of girl whom most ante-bellum authors depict has become as extinct as the dodo, if indeed she ever existed at all. So we must turn from literature, and come down from the roseate heights, whereon we thought she dwelt, to the street and home, and be as objective and concrete as possible.

II

First, the street. The other day I found myself walking a few rods behind a girl who must have been approaching sweet sixteen. She held to the middle of the broad sidewalk. It was just after four, and she was apparently on her way home from high school. We were on a long block that passed a college campus, where the students were foregathering for afternoon sports. She was not chewing gum, but was occasionally bringing some tidbit from her pocket to her mouth, taking in everything in sight, and her gait was swagger and superior. "Howdy, Billy," she called to a youth whom I fancied a classmate; and "Hello, boys," was her greeting to three more a little later.

Soon she turned on her heel and wandered back, so that I had to meet her. A glance at her comely, happy, innocent, and vividly tinted face, as I swerved to one side that she might keep the middle of the walk, almost made me feel that it would not surprise her overmuch if I stepped to the very edge of the gutter, and removed my hat, as if apologizing for trespassing on preserves that belonged to her. Had I done so, however, it might have made no difference; for I suspect that she would have remained unconscious of my very existence, although just then we were almost the only ones on the block. If I had been twenty and attractive, she would have been able to describe me to a nicety without for an instant having me in the direct focus of her vision; for we must never forget that, at this very peculiar age, nature gives to the other sex quite as great sensitiveness of indirect as of direct vision, so that they know fully as much of what falls on the periphery of their retina, as of what strikes their fovea—if not, sometimes, more.

I now felt at liberty to look at her a little more carefully. She wore a knitted hat, with hardly any brim, of a flame or bonfire hue; a henna scarf; two strings of Betty beads, of different colors, twisted together; an open short coat, with ample pockets; a skirt with vertical stripes so pleated that at the waist, it seemed very dark, but the alternate stripes of white showed progressively downward, so that, as she walked, it gave something of what physical psychologists call a flicker effect. On her right wrist were several bangles; on her left, of course, a wrist watch. Her shoes were oxfords, with a low broad heel. Her stockings were woolen and of brilliant hue. But most noticeable of all were her high overshoes or galoshes. One seemed to be turned down at the top and entirely unbuckled, while the other was fastened below and flapped about her trim ankle in a way that compelled attention. This was in January, 1922, as should

be particularly noted because, by the time this screed meets the reader's
eye, flapperdom, to be really *chic* and up-to-date, will be quite different
in some of these details. She was out to see the world and, incidentally,
to be seen of it; and as I lingered at the campus block to see the students
frolic, she passed me three times, still on her devious way home, I pre-
sume, from school.

Sheer accident had thus brought me within the range of the very specimen I sought, and perhaps a rare and extreme type; therefore, all the
more interesting.

But a deep instinct told me that I could never by any possible means
hope to get into any kind of personal *rapport* with her or even with her
like. I might have been her grandfather, and in all the world of man there
is no wider and more unbridgeable gulf than that which yawns between
me and those of my granddaughter's age. If I should try to cultivate her,
she would draw back into her shell; and to cultivate me would be the
very last of all her desires. Hence, as was only fair to her, I turned to a
third source of information about her, namely, her teachers.

They told me a large notebook full—far more than I can, and, alas!
some that I would not, repeat; so that it is puzzling to know what to
omit or even where to begin, in the tangle of incidents, traits, and judgments.

III

Let us start at random, with dancing, on which the flapper dotes as
probably never before, in all the history of the terpsichorean art, made
up of crazes as it has been, has anyone begun to do.

A good dance is as near heaven as the flapper can get and live. She
dances at noon and at recess in the school gymnasium; and if not in the
school, at the restaurants between courses, or in the recreation and rest-
rooms in factories and stores. She knows all the latest variations of the
perennial fox-trot, the ungainly contortions of the camel walk; yields with
abandon to the fascination of the tango; and if the floor is crowded, there
is always room for the languorous and infantile toddle; and the cheek-
to-cheek close formation—which one writer ascribes to the high cost of
rent nowadays, which necessitates the maximum of motion in the minimum of space—has a lure of its own, for partners must sometimes cling
together in order to move at all. Verticality of motion and, at least, the
vibrations of the "shimmy," are always possible.

High-school girls told my informant that they "park" their corsets when
they go to dances, because they have been taught by their instructors in
hygiene and physiology that to wear them is unfavorable to deep
breathing, and that this is as necessary for freedom of motion as the
gymnastic costume or the bath-suit at the seaside; and also that, to get

the best out of the exercises of the ballroom, they must not be too much or too heavily clad to be able to keep cool. To her intimates she may confess that she dispenses with corsets (a growing fashion which manufacturers of these articles already regard with alarm) lest she be dubbed "ironsides" or left a wallflower. Alas for the popularity of teachers who would limit any of these innovations, however much they may be supported by anxious and bewildered mothers, who know only the old-fashioned steps! Despite the decline of the ballet, theatrical managers who advertise for corps of stage dancers report that they are overwhelmed by crowds of applicants.

The flapper, too, has developed very decided musical tastes. If she more rarely "takes lessons" of any kind, she has many choice disks for the phonograph, and has a humming acquaintance with the most popular ditties; and if she rarely indulges in the cakewalk, she has a keen sense of ragtime and "syncopation to the thirty-second note," and her nerves are uniquely toned to jazz, with its shocks, discords, blariness, siren effects, animal and all other noises, and its heterogeneous tempos, in which every possible liberty is taken with rhythm.

Those who sell candies, ices, sodas, or "sweetened wind," are unanimous that flappers are their best customers. It somehow seems as if they could almost live on sweets; and their mothers complain that it interferes with the normality of their appetites, digestion, and nutrition generally. A girl may have acidulous tastes and love even pickles; but this is only a counterfoil. She discriminates flavors as acutely as do winetasters. She not only no longer chews gum, as she used to do, but eschews chewers of it, and even "cuts" them—for on just this point I have seen cases. But she may munch sweetmeats at the theatre, school, or even on the street. Thus the late sugar shortage was hardest on her; and how she throve so well with so short a ration of it in "the good old times" is a puzzling mystery.

If she loves sweetmeats for their own sake, why this new love of perfumery so characteristic of her age? Is her own olfactory sense suddenly much more acute, or is she now like the flowers attracting insects—but human ones? Is there a correspondingly augmented acuity in this sense in the young man? Possibly, in thus making herself fragrant she is not thinking of him at all. If she is, and he has no *flair* for it, she has made a monumental mistake. This most interesting and very important problem must be left to future investigation. At any rate, all those who sell perfumery, who were interviewed, agreed that here, too, young girls are the best customers.

Girls whose dress indicates straitened resources often lavish money upon expensive perfumes which, curiously enough nowadays, they generally prefer not pure, but mixed; so that they sometimes radiate an aura of delicate odors on the street, the components to which it would puzzle an expert to identify. The German physiologist, Jäger, finding olfaction the subtlest of all our senses, wrote two bulky volumes to prove that the soul was really a smell and concluded that love and aversion were based on emanations too subtle to reach consciousness, but which really mediated attraction and repugnance. If this is so, the soul of the young girl is far sweeter and more irradiant than it ever was before.

She dotes on jewelry, too, and her heart goes out to the rings, bracelets, bangles, beads, wrist watches, pendants, earrings, that she sees in shopwindows or on some friend or stranger. Her dream is of diamonds, rubies, sapphires, and gold; but imitations will go far to fill the aching void in her heart; and so in recent years she had made a great run on this market, as those who sell them testify.

The hair, which the Good Book calls a woman's "crown of glory" of which amorists in prose and poetry have had so much to say, and which, outside the Mongolian and Negroid races, has always been one of the chief marks of distinction between the sexes, is no longer always so. The old-fashioned demure braids once so characteristic of the budding girl are gone. Nor is the hair coiled, either high or low, at the back of the head. The medullary region long so protected is now exposed to wind and weather, either by puffs on either side, or, still more, by the Dutch cut which leaves the hair shortest here. Indeed, my barber tells me that he now shaves a space below the occiput for girls more frequently than when, in Italy, he used to freshen the tonsure of young priests above it. It is now more nearly immodest, I am told, to expose an ear than a knee, and special attention is given to the ear-lock. It is very *chic* to part the hair on one side, to keep it very smooth, as if it were plastered down on top; but on all sides of the head it must be kept tousled or combed backward *à la* Hottentot, and the more disordered it is here, the better. In all such matters, as in so many others, the girl imitates, consciously or unconsciously, her favorite movie actresses.

At least half the movie films seem almost to have been made for the flapper; and her tastes and style, if not her very code of honor, are fashioned on them. Librarians report that she reads much less since the movies came. No home or other authority can keep her away; the only amelioration is to have reels more befitting her stage of life.

I even interviewed the head of a city traffic squad, who said, as nearly as I can quote him: "When a fella speeds or breaks the rules and gets pinched, it's more than a fifty-fifty proposition he had a girl alongside, and was showin' off to her or attendin' to her, and forgettin' his machine. Some of them think it's smart to step up to Judge——, pull their roll, and peel it to pay a fine, with the girl lookin' on, or to tell her after. She sure likes joy-ridin'; and say, there was an old song about a bicycle made for two, and that's the way she wants the auto. She loves the back seat empty—no one lookin' on. They ought to have some of us out on the country roads, where they slow down and stop."

At this point the traffic became congested and took his attention, and I left him.

But I am forgetting the curriculum. In college, some subjects attract girls, and others boys, each sex sometimes monopolizing certain courses. But in high school, wherever the elective system permits choice, most girls are usually found in classes where there are most boys. Girls, too, seem fonder of cultural subjects, and less, or at least later, addicted to those that are immediately vocational. They do far better in their studies with teachers whom they like; and I have heard of an attractive unmarried male teacher who was accused by his colleagues of marking the girls in his classes too high, but whose principal had the sagacity to see that the girls did far better work for him than for any other teacher and to realize the reason why.

In the secondary school, the girl finds herself the intellectual equal of her male classmate, and far more mature at the same age in all social insights. Hence coeducation at this stage has brought her some slight disillusionment. Her boy classmates are not her ideal of the other sex, and so real lasting attachments, dating from this period, are rare. Perhaps associations and surroundings here bring also some disenchantment with her home environment, and even with her parents. But docile as she is, her heart of hearts is not in her textbooks or recitations, but always in life and persons; and she learns and adjusts herself to both with a facility and rapidity that are amazing. It is things outside her studies which seem to her, if indeed they are not in fact, far more important for her life.

IV

If any or all of the above seems extravagant, let the reader remember that I am writing so far only of the *novissima* variety of the species, which fairly burst upon the world like an insect suddenly breaking from its cocoon in full imago form; so that she is more or less a product of movies, the auto, woman suffrage, and especially, of the war. During the latter she completed her emancipation from the chaperon, and it became good patriotic form to address, give flaglets, badges, and dainties to young men in the street and, perhaps, sometimes to strike up acquaintance with them if they were in uniform. Her manners have grown a bit free-and-easy, and every vestige of certain old restraints is gone. In school she treats her male classmates almost as if sex differences did not exist. Toward him she may sometimes even seem almost aggressive. She goes to shows and walks with him evenings, and in school corridors may pat him familiarly on the back, hold him by the lapel, and elbow him in a familiar and even *de-haut-en-bas*[4] way, her teachers tell us; and they add that there is hardly a girl in the high school who does not have face-powder, comb, mirror, and perhaps rouge, in her locker, for use between sessions.

Never since civilization began has the girl in the early teens seemed so self-sufficient and sure of herself, or made such a break with the rigid traditions of propriety and convention which have hedged her in. From this, too, it follows that the tension which always exists between mothers and daughters has greatly increased, and there now sometimes seems to be almost a chasm between successive generations. If a note of loudness in dress or boisterousness in manner has crept in, and if she seems to know, or pretends to know, all that she needs to become captain of her own soul, these are really only the gestures of shaking off old fetters. Perhaps her soul has long been ripening for such a revolt, and anxious to dissipate the mystery which seemed to others to envelop it. Let us hope that she is really more innocent and healthier in mind and body because she now knows and does earlier so much that was once admissible only later, if at all.

So it is "high time" to be serious and to realize that all the above are only surface phenomena, and that the real girl beneath them is, after all, but little changed; or that, if she is changed, it is on the whole for the better. Beneath all this new self-revelation, she still remains a mystery. She is so insecure in all her new assurance that it may be shattered by a slight which others do not notice; or some uncomplimentary remark by a mate may humble her pride in the dust. The sublime selfishness, of which the flapper is so often accused, which makes her accept and demand to be served by parents and all about her whom she can subject; her careless responsibilities, which render her unconscious of all the trouble she makes, or the worries which others feel for her present and future; and the fact that she never seems to realize what it means to clean up after herself, easily alternate with the extreme desire to serve, herself, and to lavish attention upon those whom she really likes. Despite her mien of independence, she is stingingly sensitive to every breath of good-and-ill-will; and if she has shattered old conventions, she has not gone wrong; and if she knows about things of which she must still often pretend to be ignorant, she is thereby only the more fortified against temptation.

The flapper, too, can be cruel, and often is so, to other girls. She ought not to be, and, it would seem, does not want to be, for she knows full well from her own experience how slights and innuendoes sting and burn. Perhaps she feels deep down in her soul that she is thus helping to toughen the fibre of her mates, to enable them to meet better the slings and arrows of outrageous fortune, which they will encounter later in life.

The metamorphosis of boys into maturity is easy to observe, for nature hangs out signs that all may read—the first thistle-down of a beard, the mutation of the voice, very ostensive declarations of independence in thought and action, etc. Every known race of primitive man initiates its pubescent youth, often by elaborate rites—usually significant of a new birth—into manhood and the life of the tribe; but there are relatively few such rites for girls at the corresponding physiological age; although the changes they undergo are perhaps yet more transforming, and beset with more dangers, both of arrest and of perversion.

There are a few buds in the past who have let themselves with abandon into print, like Marie Bashkirtseff and poor Mary MacLane; while other few have remembered and written voluminously of this stage in their own life, like George Sand the author of *Una Mary*; and the inmost movings of the soul of a few more have been overheard by accident, as in *A Young Girl's Diary*. Some of these revealers of femininity in its callow ephebic stages have been called traitors to their sex, betraying what should be its most guarded secrets in a way likely to tarnish its glamour for the other sex. But the mental and moral abnormalities here met with have been far more fully explored in ways that show that, at this coming-out-stage, the modern female ephebe comes nearer than any human being ever did before to being "all mankind's epitome." She has not entirely laid aside certain boyish, and even childish, traits, but the floodgates of heredity are open again, and instincts from the immemorial past are surging up. Of course, she seems a bundle of inconsistencies, although there is a fundamental unity underneath them all. She is simply like a climbing vine in the stages of circumnutation, before it has found the support by which it can raise itself toward the sun. Curiously enough, we have several statistical surveys which show that the vast majority of adult women look back upon the early teens as the richest stage of all their life, especially in the feelings, which are the voice of extinct generations, while the intellect is a more personal acquisition.

V

One of the flapper's chief traits is a passion for secrecy, and this is one reason why her teachers, parents, pastor, doctor, really know so very little about her, for she has developed a *modus vivendi*[5] with each that often disarms suspicion of concealment. Her real inner life is being evolved far beyond their ken. Her very anatomy and physiological development suggest involution and her crepuscular soul is in an ingrowing stage. With her intimates she always has secrets, which it is treason to friendship to betray. A little younger, she invents, or even pretends, secrets as bonds of intimacy, or gives words an esoteric meaning. And has signs and badges which no one but her chosen few understands. So, too, she may come to believe that others have secrets which they try to keep from her, particularly about vital themes, which she feels she has a right to know. Thus, if too much baulked, she may listen, or imagine hidden meanings which do not exist.

The demure miss who sits silently at our table and in our drawing-room while we talk, who goes through all the paces of schoolwork and social observances set for her, is not the real girl, and she knows it; for her true self is all the more securely masked by conforming to what we expect of her. Her imagination is in the most active stages of creative evolution, although its activities are often so submerged beneath the threshold of consciousness, that she is herself not aware of its fecund spontaneity. She is all the while developing swift *apercus*[6] full of insights and judgments about persons; and she is taking attitudes, for she is in the springtide of sentiment and her ideality, to which the world owes so much, could not attain its goal if it were not more or less veiled.

Thus she is not what she seems, and with but a slight tincture of pathology, the passion to deceive may become dominant. The Fox sisters, who gave the first impulse to spiritism in this country, and the five Creery sisters, séances with whom filled the early proceedings of the English Society for Psychic Research, were in the early teens, and there have been scores of such masked hystericals, who fooled everybody. The Watseka Wonder was too much for even the astute and detective mind of the late Professor Hodgson; and in reviewing the merry dances which budding girls have led psychiatrists, especially in France a few decades ago, I concluded that, wherever a brand new theory of hysteria, epilepsy or telepathy was promulgated by any of them, we should first of all follow the maxim *Cherchez le tendron*.[7] This vast disparity between her inner and outer life really compels the girl to feign what is not, and to dissimulate what is.

She is in the most interesting stage of the long and complex process of getting ready to love and be loved. It is already several years since all boys ceased to seem crude, oafish, and altogether inconvenient, and began—at least, one or two of them—to be interesting. She has also pretty well passed the stage of amatory fetishism, when she was prone to dote on some single feature, trait, or act, and feel a degree of aversion for others for which nothing could compensate. She is just learning to perform her supreme selective function of passing judgment on personalities as a whole, and with their *ensemble*[8] of qualities. A small but rather constant percentage of girls of high-school age evolve, more or less unconsciously, an ideal hero, or make one of some older youth; and this sometimes seems to serve as a defense against "falling for" even the best specimen of the other sex among her acquaintances of her own age. George Eliot rather crassly says that for some years a girl's every act may tend to provoke proposals. But, if she wants attention, she flees from it, if she detects serious signs of intention. She has no idea of marrying till she has had her innocent fling, or perhaps tried her hand at self-support. Intuition warns her of the danger of loving or being loved with abandon.

A few years before she was pryingly curious. Eight ninth-grade girls signed their names, round-robin-wise, to a request to be told "truly where we come from." The teacher in her perplexity took the petition to the principal who passed it on to the superintendent; and the latter referred it to the school board, where it has rested. This was some years ago, and these girls have long since found their answer.

Eager as she is to know, however, she is really repelled if knowledge comes in an improper form. How she hates those who offend! And if she feels the least vestige of real fascination, how she reproaches, and perhaps even fears for, herself. If she becomes aware of the tender passion burgeoning in her own soul, she guards it as the most sacred of all her secrets; and towards the object of it she may affect indifference or even rudeness, perhaps repulsing common courtesies as if they were meant to be advances.

If, despite all these instinctive reluctances which kind old mother nature inspires, she loses her moorings and is swept precociously into a great love, the death-thought is always near; for in the primer of virginity Eros and Thanatos are mystic twins. The supreme affirmation of life, if precocious, brings a compensating thought of its negation. She may even dream of going to heaven by water, which statistics show is the favorite route at this age. She may imagine herself a beautiful corpse, laid out with flowers, while mourning friends weep and praise her, realizing at last that she was not appreciated while he, the most inconsolable of them all, is dissolved in tears, vowing to devote his life henceforth to the memory of her.

Girls often idealize one candidate for their affections after another, in rapid succession. One frankly told me that she had been in love with a different one every school term, but none had survived the long vacation. How little a generally desirable young man suspects the havoc he may wreak between a pair of girl soul-mates by partiality to the one and ever so little neglect of the other! Indeed, so tinglingly sensitive are girls that even the changing feelings toward mates to whom they are relatively indifferent contribute their quota of fluctuations of mood, which seem so unaccountable to onlookers, when, in fact, all such alternations have a very real and sufficient reason.

Thrice happy the girl who, through these years of seething and ferment, has a father whom she can make the embodiment of her ideals; for he is, all unconsciously, the pattern to which her future lover and husband must conform. But even here there are dangers; for if her fondness for her father is too intense, or unduly prolonged, this makes it impossible for her ever to be happy if mated to a man not in the father image. She may even be a little motherly toward her parents, although her attitude toward her mother is infinitely complex. While we almost never find any of the jealousy toward her which Freudians stress, there is, especially in these days of sudden emancipation from the conventions in vogue a generation ago, an unprecedented tension between mother and daughter, which may be reinforced if the former has failed to give certain instruction in life-problems. Thus, occasionally a girl's devotion to her mother, if it is excessive, may be due to a blind instinct to compensate for thoughts and feelings toward her that she deems not truly filial; and if she has caught herself in a mood of hostility, she may overwhelm her mother with attentions that are embarrassing.

VI

The outburst of growth in the earliest teens, which make the average girl, for a very brief period, slightly taller and heavier than the boy (an increment which, in its maximal year, amounts to nearly three inches in height and ten or twelve pounds in weight), involves many sudden changes. The sudden upthrust that brings her to the level of grown-ups and sometimes enables the girl of fifteen or sixteen (she will never be a third of an inch taller than she is on her seventeenth birthday) to look down upon her mother, causes her to be taken for older than she is, and may give her some sense of insufficiency in the new relationships to adults thus thrust upon her. She feels her height, perhaps awkwardly, and must affect the ways of young womanhood when she is yet a child in her heart and mind. Perhaps she does not assert her height, and tends to stoop a little, impairing the development of vital organs. It is curious, by the way, to note that, like plants, she grows tall fastest in the spring, and gains in weight and thickness most in the autumn, and that growth in the latter dimension, which comes a trifle later, is not infrequently lost in this country and England, giving us the slender Gibson type.

At the same time, her mental development is by leaps and bounds. She matures more now in one year than she will in five during her twenties, or ten in later years. In this development she still further distances boys. This has the curious result of narrowing the age-scale of her intimacies. She has little use for girls of less psychological age, and is never less sympathetic with young children and babies; and on entering high school, she not only lays aside many former interests, but even "cuts" those who persist in certain games and occupations quite permissible for eighth- and ninth-graders. As she draws more closely to those in her own state, she lessens vital contact with those a little older, unless she has a "crush" for some upper-class individual. Hence the sharp demarcations through secondary and academic grades.

Thus despite the uniformitizing effect of fashions, the contagion of fads, and the intense imitativeness of this stage, individuality is being developed, and the new and ostensive assertiveness has in it the promise and potency of a new and truer womanhood. In all the long struggle for emancipation, sometimes called the war of sex against sex, woman has, and perhaps, necessarily, laid aside for the time some other most distinctive traits, and competed with man along his own lines, and has perhaps grown thereby a little masculine. But true progress demands that sex-distinctions be pushed to the uttermost, and that women become more feminine and men more virile. This need modern feminism has failed to recognize; but it is just this which flapperdom is now asserting. These girls not only accept, but glory in their sex as such, and are giving free course to its native impulses. They may be the leaders in the complete emancipation of woman from the standards man has made for her. Up to this age our Binet-Simon tests can grade and mark, at least for intelligence, but here they baulk, stammer, and diverge.

The flapper's new sophistication is thus superficial. Her new self-consciousness is really naive, and in her affectations she is simply trying out all the assortments of temperamental types, dispositions, and traits of character, as she often tries out styles of handwriting before she settles upon one. This is all because hers is the most vital and most rapidly developing psyche in all the world. The evolutionary stages of flapperdom are so many, and they succeed each other so fast, and are so telescoped together that we cannot yet determine the order of their sequence, and all my glimpses are only random snapshots of the wonderful quadrennium, the first four teens.

She accepts the confirmation, and perhaps even the conversion, that the church prescribes; but her heart is set on this world and not on the next. She conforms with the more interest to the "coming-out" customs of society; but these are now much belated, for in all essentials she came out unaided, and the age of her legal majority she deems too late. Once it was commonly held that those who were precocious would become blasé later; but if there ever was danger here, it exists no longer. In fact, civilization itself, and all our hope that mankind may attain superhumanity, depends on the prolongation, enrichment, and safeguarding of the interval between pubescence and ripe nubility.

What a reversal of ancient and traditional mores it would be if the flapper, long repressed by so many taboos, were now to become the pioneer and leader of her sex to a new dispensation, and to give the world its very best illustration of the trite but pregnant slogan, *Das ewig Weibliche sieht uns hinan.*[9] She has already set fashions in attire, and even in manners, some of which her elders have copied, and have found not only sensible, but rejuvenating. Under the mannish ways which she sometimes affects, she really wants her femininity. And her exuberance gives it a new charm. The new liberties she takes with life are contagious, and make us wonder anew whether we have not all been servile to precedent, and slaves to institutions that need to be refitted to human nature, and whether the flapper may not, after all, be the bud of a new and better womanhood.

NOTES

1. *Americana* usually refers to some aspect of American culture rather than to a person. *Novissima* means "newest." Hall is calling the flapper the latest thing in American culture.

2. Hall is making a mild joke about the difference between these two terms. To the Germans the flapper is a *backfisch*, or fish prepared to eat. It would be nicer to think, he says, that they really meant *bachfisch*, or the fish he describes as hatching in fresh water and then going down to sea.

3. The literal meaning of the Latin is "unknown land." It can refer to anything new and strange.

4. This French idiom is perhaps best translated as "condescending."

5. The Latin means "way of living." A *modus vivendi* is a way of getting along—of coping with a situation, adjusting to it.

6. This French plural is best translated as "surveys."

7. The French expression *cherchez la femme* goes back to detective fiction. It means "find the woman," supposedly the first step in solving a crime. Later anti-feminine cynics applied it to any sort of situation. Hall has already used *tendron*, the French word for *bud*, as an equivalent for *flapper*. So *cherchez le tendron* means "find the flapper."

8. This French term means "collection," "assembly."

9. This German expression is perhaps best translated nonliterally as "The eternal feminine will always be beyond our comprehension."

SPECIAL ASSIGNMENT

The following words from "Flapper Americana Novissima" are arranged according to the section in which they appear. Select five of them
and look up the dictionary meanings. Now go back to where the words
appear in the text and rewrite the pertinent passages in your own words.
Do you like your version better? Try reading your version to your classmates to get their reactions.

Section I

lexicographer

pubescent

labyrinthine

ante-bellum

dodo

roseate

Section II

periphery

retina

fovea

screed

rapport

Section III

terpsichorean

verticality

acidulous

counterfoil

eschew

physiologist

olfactory

emanations

irradiant

amorists

medullary

occiput

tonsure

amelioration

sagacity

Section IV

imago

ostensive

callow

ephebic

Section V

crepuscular

fecund

astute

promulgated

feign

dissimulate

amatory

fetishism

crassly

burgeoning

precociously

Eros

Thanatos

Section VI

increment

maximal

demarcations

psyche

quadrennium

precocious

blasé

mores

trite

rejuvenated

STUDY QUESTIONS

1. Are Daisy Buchanan and Jordan Baker slightly older flappers than those described by Hall? What do they have in common with flappers? How are they different?

2. Do you think it likely that the flappers G. Stanley Hall describes could ever grow up to be like Mary Dillon? Why or why not? Would Hall approve of them if they did? What life roles do you think Hall envisions for most women?

3. Is the flapper very different from the modern girl her age? If so, how?

4. In what ways is the flapper similar to modern girls?

5. Are there things about the flapper that would be true of girls in any age? If so, what are they?

6. Are there things about Daisy Buchanan and Jordan Baker that Nick Carraway finds unattractive? If so, are these things what one expects of flappers?

7. None of the heroines in Fitzgerald's major works of fiction are career oriented. This is true in spite of the fact that Sheilah Graham, who served as the model for the heroine in *The Love of the Last Tycoon*, was very career oriented. After reading *The Great Gatsby*, take a guess as to why this might be so.

8. Imagine Tom Buchanan doing business with Mary Dillon. How would it go?

9. Imagine Nick Carraway doing the same thing. What would be his reaction? Think carefully about his attitude toward women.

10. If you are female, imagine yourself being told that you can have a promotion if you promise not to get married. How would you react? If you are male, imagine yourself telling a female employee the same thing. What reaction would you expect?

11. In what ways do you think Mary Dillon differs from modern business women?

12. Mary Dillon seems to feel that her long wait for a promotion was justified. How do you feel?

13. Gatsby's career, for a time at least, is a kind of success story. Contrast it with Mary Dillon's.

14. What are the most serious differences between Daisy Buchanan and Mary Dillon?

15. How do you think Mary Dillon would react to Tom Buchanan's social circle?

16. Both Gertrude Ederle and Jordan Baker are athletes. From what you have just read, what do you think are the differences between them? In what ways are they similar?

17. Compare and contrast the attitudes toward girls and women in the articles by Bennett and Hall with the attitude in the *Literary Digest* article.

18. Carrie Chapman Catt is quoted as saying that the American woman of her time (the 1920s) was a much better physical specimen "than she was two generations ago." How do you think girls of today compare with their grandmothers and great-grandmothers?

19. Catt also says of the American girl that "she is ashamed to be ill." Do you think this is true now? Explain.

20. How do you think Nick Carraway would have responded to Gertrude Ederle's achievements? Explain.

21. Would Daisy have responded differently? Explain.

22. Do you think Jordan Baker would have welcomed Gertrude Ederle as a fellow athlete? Explain.

23. Would Tom Buchanan approve of Gertrude Ederle? Would he feel threatened by her success? Defend your answer.

24. How would G. Stanley Hall have classified Gertrude Ederle? As a superflapper? Look carefully at what he says about male and female roles.

25. Gertrude Ederle was nineteen when she swam the Channel. Does she seem mature for her age? Immature? Defend your answer.

26. How would reactions to Gertrude Ederle be different now from what they were in 1926?

27. Has women's success in sports changed any basic social attitudes? If so, what attitudes?

28. Do you know any flappers? What about them makes them flappers? Be specific.

29. If you are female, would you be insulted if someone called you a flapper? Why or why not?

TOPICS FOR WRITTEN OR ORAL EXPLORATION

1. G. Stanley Hall's style is not a good model for a modern writer, but as an exercise, conduct this experiment. Pick what you think is an

important or exciting scene in *The Great Gatsby* and rewrite it using Hall's style and attitudes. If you dislike Hall's writing, here is your chance to get even.

2. Hall says that "true progress demands that sex-distinction be pushed to the uttermost, and that women become more feminine and men more virile." This thinking was typical of his generation. Was he right or wrong about this? If he was right, what would that say about women's liberation since the 1960s?

3. Look at the hotel room scene in chapter 7 of *The Great Gatsby*. This is a crucial scene, because it is here that Gatsby loses Daisy to Tom, although Gatsby does not realize it. It has been suggested that Daisy goes back to Tom because she realizes how unstable Gatsby's world and finances really are, and that she needs the wealth and security she gets from Tom. Look very carefully at the exchanges between Tom, Daisy, and Gatsby, and come to your own conclusion. Is Fitzgerald really saying something here about the nature of marriage?

4. Gatsby and Daisy go back from the hotel in the same car. This is the last time they see each other. What do you think they said to each other before Myrtle Wilson was killed? Create your own version of the conversation.

5. What do you think Gatsby and Daisy said to each other after Myrtle Wilson was killed? Create your own version.

SUGGESTIONS FOR FURTHER READING

The Fitzgerald biographies listed in Chapter 3 are excellent sources for studying the relationship between F. Scott Fitzgerald and Zelda. The following books are more generally related to the position of women at the time *The Great Gatsby* was written.

Fryer, Sara Beebe. *Fitzgerald's New Women: Harbingers of Change*. Ann Arbor: UMI Research Press, 1988.

Mayfield, Sara. *The Constant Circle: H. L. Mencken and His Friends*. New York: Delacorte Press, 1968. This book describes a woman's social group in Montgomery, Alabama. Included in it were Zelda Sayre, actress Tallulah Bankhead, and the novelist Sarah Hardt. Mayfield treats the Fitzgeralds' marital difficulties primarily from Zelda's point of view.

Milford, Nancy. *Zelda: A Biography*. New York: Harper and Row, 1970.

Sochen, June. *Herstory: A Woman's View of American History*. New York: Alfred Publishing, 1974.

Woloch, Nancy. *Women and the American Experience*. New York: Alfred A. Knopf, 1984.

To get an idea of the kinds of clothes Fitzgerald's characters would have worn, see *Everyday Fashions of the Twenties as Pictured in Sears and Other Catalogs* (New York: Dover, 1981), edited by Stella Blum, who served as Curator of the Costume Institute of the Metropolitan Museum of Art in New York City.

5 _____

Why Not Be Rich? Money in the 1920s

One of the main themes of *The Great Gatsby* is the attitude of its characters—especially Gatsby—toward money. From the poem about the gold-hatted lover that serves as an epigraph, to Nick Carraway's meditations on the green light at the conclusion, money symbolism runs through the novel. Gatsby says Daisy's voice is "full of money," and worships the green, money-colored light across the bay where Daisy lives as though it were the Holy Grail. Even minor details of the novel remind the reader of money. The man who sells Tom Buchanan and Myrtle Wilson a mongrel pup is said to look like John D. Rockefeller.

Gatsby's love of Daisy is partly based on the glamor he associates with her money, and he pursues her by becoming wealthy himself. His passion for Daisy blends with earlier desires for financial success going all the way back to the daily schedule he established as a boy. His dream is completely misguided. The wealthy in this novel—Daisy and Tom Buchanan—turn out to be empty, worthless people. Through Nick Carraway's disillusionment as he observes Gatsby's failure and destruction, Fitzgerald is commenting on American attitudes toward money and success in the 1920s. When Nick sees how these attitudes destroy Gatsby, he is warned off adopting them himself. He is left, however, with nothing with which to replace them.

American popular culture at this time was obsessed with rapid and easy acquisition of wealth. It tended to make heroes out of almost anyone who had become wealthy, in almost any field. The *American Magazine*, for example, carried at least one success story nearly every month, and often more. A typical issue (August 1924) contained the success story of a minister—"From a Tiny Cottage Church to a Temple on Broadway"—and the success story of an executive of an engineering corporation—"This 'Bad Boy' Fooled the Town Prophets." Advertising executive Bruce Barton wrote *The Man Nobody Knows* to convince the world that Jesus was a husky, two-fisted natural leader, salesman, and advertising man. His career, according to Barton, was a masterpiece of executive and advertising brilliance.

A careful reader of *The Great Gatsby* will see that Fitzgerald thought this single-minded pursuit of wealth could lead to disaster, both psychological and material. One need only remember what happens to Gatsby. Although no one knew it when *The Great Gatsby* appeared in 1925, the United States was headed for one of the worst disasters in its history—the Great Depression of the 1930s.

Fitzgerald was one of those badly hurt by the Depression. The public turned away from the subject matter of his fiction, seeming to feel half-consciously that it was now paying for the wildness and dissipations of the Jazz Age. It wanted fiction about social problems, about slums, and about strikes in steel mills and coal mines. Fitzgerald was thought of as a frivolous writer who dealt with the frivolous rich. Only a few intelligent readers understood that he was one of the most brilliant analysts of the values of his time.

Fitzgerald's later life and much of his later work became a commentary on his own earlier life and the life he had described in his fiction. By the 1930s he was alcoholic and suffered first from diabetes and tuberculosis, and finally from the heart condition that killed him in 1940. His wife had become schizophrenic; with each new episode of illness, it became less likely that she would ever be well. He was deeply in debt and owed money for his wife's confinement in good sanitariums and for his daughter's education. He managed to pay most of his debts by writing for films, work he did not like but tried his best to do well. Very little of what he wrote for Hollywood was ever used, but he was well paid.

A story published in 1931, "Babylon Revisited," closely resembles his own life, and it also reflects on the world he described in *The Great Gatsby*. Its hero, Charlie Wales, quit work in the late twenties and lived off the money he made playing the stock market. While he did this, he and his wife lived a wild alcoholic life in Paris. His wife died after he locked her out one winter night, and he went into a sanitarium to dry out. Relatives were given custody of his daughter. Wales, now living a sober life, returns to Paris in hope of reclaiming his daughter. The city has become ghastly for him. Some misfortune or breakdown has overtaken almost everyone he once knew there. Nick's description in chapter 4 of those who attend Gatsby's parties foreshadows what Wales now finds in Paris. Many of the characters at Gatsby's parties have strange and unhappy fates. Similarly, Charlie Wales finds that his old friends have lost both their health and their money.

Few things were more typical of the 1920s than stock speculation and the collapse of the market in 1929. Experts still disagree about how important the crash was. Some believe the Great Depression had already started without the public realizing it and that the crash only made it worse. Others think the crash itself was the main cause of the Depression. But regardless of what caused it, the crash marked a symbolic turning point in American life.

The crash ruined many lives. Imagine a situation where many investors have bought stocks on, say, 30 percent margin. This means that they have paid 30 percent of the price and owe the rest. Then imagine a situation where a bank has accepted the stock as security for a loan to buy more stock, and in some cases is carrying the loan balance on the stock already bought. Suddenly, beginning on October 24, 1929, everyone wants to sell stocks and no one will buy. The stock has become worthless. The holder of the stock has lost much more than the money he has invested. He has lost all the money he owes on the stock. The bank, holding worthless stock as security for a loan that cannot be repaid, may go broke. As the failing bank tries to call in loans to save itself, businesses everywhere may go under. Depositors who have nothing to do with the stock market may be wiped out when the bank goes broke. Money deposited in savings accounts in most banks is now protected up to a certain amount by federal insurance, but in the 1920s bank deposits were not insured.

Most of the really wild speculation on the stock market occurred between 1927 and 1929. Until 1927 the rising stock prices were fairly close to real increases in the value of the companies whose stock was traded. After that, some stock prices remained about the same, and a few even declined, but others skyrocketed. Share prices of General Electric stock rose over 300 percent between March 1928 and September 1929, and the price of Anaconda Copper stock rose 240 percent over the same period. It was extremely unlikely that such companies had increased that much in productivity or in real value in that length of time. People who had bought overvalued stocks on margin at high prices were in a very dangerous position.

Many people who thought they were making sound investments for their old age found that their savings were wiped out, and many found themselves in debt because they still owed money on stocks that had become worthless. Many people lost homes and cars. Many businesses failed, and people who had never had trouble finding work now could not find any. Across the United States many college students got messages telling them to come home. Their families had lost their money and could no longer support them. Bright young people who had planned on going to college sometimes found that they could not even finish high school. They had to take whatever work they could find just to survive and to help support their families.

The misery that came with the Depression changed people's attitudes. They thought much more about politics and economics than they had before. They resented the rich more than they had before, and blamed the rich for the Depression. One of the many changes was in the attitude toward literature. People began to think that Fitzgerald's writing about the rich was thoughtless and showed a lack of social responsibility. Nothing could have been further from the truth. Fitzgerald had described the world of the twenties on the way down to the disaster of the Depression.

Although published after *The Great Gatsby* was written, the articles that follow illustrate themes that run throughout Fitzgerald's work. The first is a seemingly reasonable invitation to all Americans to become independently wealthy by middle age through stock investment. The second, published about three months later, is an account of the 1929 crash. Fitzgerald was always aware of his culture's preoccupation with easy financial success, but even in his earliest work there is a sense of impending doom, a sense that something is fundamentally wrong, a sense of something indefinably menacing. It would be silly to claim that Fitzgerald prophesied the crash of the stock market, just as it would be a crude over-simplification of his very sensitive fiction to say that all he was doing was lecturing his readers about being overly concerned with material success. But in spite of that, readers aware of the boom of the twenties and the ensuing Depression will see much more in Fitzgerald's fiction than they otherwise would.

JOHN J. RASKOB

The following interview expresses a common belief of the late 1920s—a belief that easy wealth and nearly unlimited prosperity were available to anyone who would take them. A very powerful and influential figure, John J. Raskob was one of the originators of a kind of credit buying that made possible the phenomenal financial expansion of the 1920s. After World War I many Americans wanted to buy automobiles, and the manufacturers and salesmen commonly used hard-sell techniques on hesitant buyers. But few people had enough cash to buy a car outright. Banks lent money on real estate and on businesses—on things that were likely to hold their value or even increase in value.

Raskob, an executive at General Motors Corporation, worked with William Durant, the founder of General Motors, to create General Motors Acceptance Corporation, which enabled the ordinary American to buy an automobile on credit, as most of us do today. Ford was forced to do the same thing. From buying cars on credit, it was an easy step to buying other large items on credit. Based largely on consumer credit, the boom of the twenties was on.

Raskob had first been an executive with the Du Pont Company, and had gone to General Motors when the Du Pont Company bought the corporation. In most ways he was very conservative. He backed Republican presidential candidate Calvin Coolidge in 1924 and conservative Democrat Al Smith in 1928. His recommendations about handling trusts in this article are in one way similar to his recommendations for financing automobiles. They enable someone with little money to get involved by using credit.

An ordinary person with a small amount of surplus money, he argues, will ordinarily get little long-term benefit from his money. To save it is to let it stagnate. To buy bonds in companies would mean taking all the risks involved in investing in a company's stock without the possibility of benefiting from the company's growth, as one would if the value of the stock increased. If the company were to go broke, both the bonds and the stocks would be worthless. But the bond will never be worth more than its face value, no matter how successful the company is.

Stocks, then, are the best investment. But the average citizen is too ignorant to invest wisely. What he can do is put small sums of money in a trust regularly and let an expert make the investment decisions. In order to discipline himself, this ordinary citizen can arrange to finance his trust investments with credit, and pay them off just as he pays off his car loans. By the time this person is middle aged, his income from stocks in the trust will match the earnings from his job.

When the stock market crashed in 1929, these trusts were being created at the rate of one a day. One thing Raskob does not mention is that, instead of investing all their money in the stock market, many trusts invested in other trusts. Imagine a trust which invests in a trust which invests in a trust which invests in a trust. Now imagine that in all these trusts people have been investing borrowed money, not just their savings. Now imagine that the last trust in this series loses heavily in the crash. A chain reaction wipes out all the trusts. The investors no longer have real investments. Now they have debts instead.

President Hoover thought the stock market was unhealthy and did what he could to get editors and advisors to discourage speculation. Alexander Dana Noyes, financial editor of the *New York Times*, predicted the crash, and so did George Soule, a financial expert writing for the *New Republic*. But many others, like Raskob, remained optimistic until disaster struck.

FROM SAMUEL CROWTHER, "EVERYBODY OUGHT TO BE RICH:
AN INTERVIEW WITH JOHN J. RASKOB"
(Ladies' Home Journal, August 1929, pp. 9, 36)*

Being rich is, of course, a comparative status. A man with a million dollars used to be considered rich, but so many people have at least that much in these days, or are earning incomes in excess of a normal return from a million dollars, that a millionaire does not cause any comment.

Fixing a bulk line to define riches is a pointless performance. Let us rather say that a man is rich when he has an income from invested capital which is sufficient to support him and his family in a decent and comfortable manner—to give as much support, let us say, as has ever been given by his earnings. That amount of prosperity ought to be attainable by anyone. A greater share will come to those who have greater ability.

It seems to me to be a primary duty for people to make it their business to understand how wealth is produced and not to take their ideas from writers and speakers who have the gift of words but not the gift of ordinary common sense. Wealth is not created in dens of iniquity, and it is much more to the point to understand what it is all about than to listen to the expounding of new systems which at the best can only make worse the faults in our present system.

It is quite true that wealth is not so evenly distributed as it ought to be. And part of the reason for the unequal distribution is the lack of systematic investment and also the lack of even moderately sensible investment.

One class of investors saves money and puts it into savings banks or other mediums that pay only a fixed interest. Such funds are valuable, but they do not lead to wealth. A second class tries to get rich all at once, and buys any wildcat security that comes along with the promise of immense returns. A third class holds that the return from interest is not enough to justify savings, but at the same time has too much sense to buy false stocks—and so saves nothing at all. Yet all the while wealth has been there for the taking.

The common stocks of this country have in the past ten years increased enormously in value because the business of the country has increased. Ten thousand dollars invested ten years ago in the common stock of General Motors would now be worth more than a million and a half dollars. And General Motors is only one of many first-class industrial corporations. It may be said that this is a phenomenal increase and that conditions are going to be different in the next ten years. That prophecy may be true, but it is not founded on experience. In my opinion the wealth of the country is bound to increase at a very rapid rate. The rapidity of the rate will be determined by the increase in consumption, and under wise investment plans the consumption will steadily increase.

We Have Scarcely Started

Now anyone may regret that he or she did not have ten thousand dollars ten years ago and did not put it into General Motors or some other good company—and sigh over a lost opportunity. Anyone who firmly believes that the opportunities are all closed and that from now on the country will get worse instead of better is welcome to the opinion and to whatever increment it will bring. I think that we have scarcely started, and I have thought so for many years.

In conjunction with others I have been interested in creating and directing at least a dozen trusts for investment in equity securities. This plan of equity investments is no mere theory with me. The first of these trusts was started in 1907 and the others in the years immediately following. Under all of these the plan provided for the saving of fifteen dollars per month for investment in equity securities only. There were no stocks bought on margin, no money borrowed, nor any stocks bought for a quick turn or resale. All stocks with few exceptions have been bought and held as permanent investments. The fifteen dollars was saved every month and the dividends from the stocks purchased were kept in the trust and reinvested. Three of these trusts are now twenty years old. Fifteen dollars per month equals one hundred and eighty dollars per year. In twenty years, therefore, the total savings amounted to thirty-six hundred dollars. Each of these three trusts is now worth well in excess of eighty thousand dollars. Invested at 6 percent interest, this eighty thousand dollars would give the trust beneficiary an annual income of four hundred dollars per month, which ordinarily would represent more than the earning power of the beneficiary, because had he been able to earn as much as four hundred dollars per month he could have saved more than fifteen dollars.

Suppose a man marries at the age of twenty-three and begins a regular saving of fifteen dollars a month—and almost anyone who is employed can do it if he tries. If he invests in good common stocks and allows the dividends and rights to accumulate, he will at the end of twenty years have at least eighty thousand dollars and an income from investments of around four hundred dollars a month. He will be rich. And because anyone can do that I am firm in my belief that anyone not only can be rich but ought to be rich.

The obstacles to being rich are two: The trouble of saving, and the trouble of finding a medium for investment.

If Tom is known to have two hundred dollars in the savings bank then everyone is out to get it for some absolutely necessary purpose. More than likely his wife's sister will eventually find the emergency to draw it forth. But if he does withstand the attacks, what good will the money do him? The interest he receives is so small that he has no incentive to save, and since the whole is under his jurisdiction he can depend only upon his own will to save. To save in any such fashion requires a stronger will than the normal.

If he thinks of investing in some stock he has nowhere to turn for advice. He is not big enough to get much attention from his banker, and he has not enough money to go to a broker—or at least he thinks that he does not.

Suppose he has a thousand dollars; the bank can only advise him to buy a bond, for the officer will not take the risk of advising a stock and probably has not the experience anyway to give such advice. Tom can get really adequate attention only from some man who has a worthless security to sell, for then all of Tom's money will be profit. The plan that I have had in mind for several years grows out of the success of the plans that we have followed for the executives in the General Motors and the Du Pont companies. In 1923, in order to give the executives of General Motors a greater interest in their work, we organized the Managers Securities Company, made up of eighty senior and junior executives. This company bought General Motors common stock to the market value of thirty-three million dollars. The executives paid five million dollars in cash and borrowed twenty-eight million dollars. The stock holders of the Managers Securities Company are not stockholders of General Motors. They own stock in a company which owns stock in General Motors, so that, as far as General Motors is concerned, the stock is voted as a block according to the instructions of the directors of the Managers Securities Company. This supplies an important interest which can exercise a large influence in shaping the policies of General Motors.

From $25,000 to a Million

The holdings of the members in these securities are adjusted in cases of men leaving the employ of the company. The plan of the Managers Securities Company contemplates no dissolution of that company, so that its holdings of General Motors stock will always be *en bloc*. The plan has been enormously successful. And much of the success of General Motors Corporation has been due to the executives' having full responsibility and receiving financial rewards commensurate with that responsibility.

The participation in the Managers Securities Company was arranged in accordance with the position and salary of the executive. Minimum participation required a cash payment of twenty-five thousand dollars when the Managers Securities Company was organized. That minimum participant is now worth more than one million dollars.

Recently I have been advocating the formation of an equity securities corporation; that is, a corporation that will invest in common stocks only under proper and careful supervision. This company will have the common stocks of first-class industrial corporations and issue its own stock certificates against them. This stock will be offered from time to time at a price to correspond exactly with the value of the assets of the corporation and all profits will go to the stockholders. The directors will be men of outstanding character, reputation and integrity. At regular intervals—say quarterly—the whole financial record of the corporation will be published together with all its holdings and the cost thereof. The corporation will be owned by the public and with every transaction public. I am not at all interested in a private investment trust. The company would not be permitted to borrow money or go into any debt.

In addition to this company, there should be organized a discount company on the same lines as the finance companies of the motor concerns to be used to sell stocks of the investing corporation on the installment plan. If Tom had two hundred dollars, this company would lend him three hundred dollars and thus enable him to buy five hundred dollars of the equity securities investment company stock, and Tom could arrange to pay off the loan just as he pays off his motor car loan. When finished he would own outright five hundred dollars of equity stock. That would take his savings out of the free-will class and put them into the compulsory-payment class and his savings would no longer be fair game for relatives, for swindlers or for himself.

People pay for their motor car loans. They will also pay their loans contracted to secure their share in the nation's business. And in the kind of company suggested every increase in the value and every right would go to the benefit of the stockholders and be reflected in the price and earning power of the stock. They would share absolutely in the nation's prosperity.

Constructive Saving

The effect of all this would, to my mind, be very far reaching. If Tom bought five hundred dollars' worth of stock he would be helping some manufacturer to buy a new lathe or a new machine of some kind, which would add to the wealth of the country, and Tom, by participating in the profits of this machine, would be in a position to buy more goods and cause a demand for more machines. Prosperity is in the nature of an endless chain and we can break it only by our own refusal to see what it is.

Everyone ought to be rich, but it is out of the question to make people rich in spite of themselves.

The millennium is not at hand. One cannot have all play and no work. But it has been sufficiently demonstrated that many of the old and supposedly conservative maxims are as untrue as the radical notions. We can appraise things as they are.

Everyone by this time ought to know that nothing can be gained by stopping the progress of the world and dividing up everything—there would not be enough to divide, in the first place, and in the second place, most of the world's wealth is not in such form it can be divided.

The socialist theory of division is, however, no more irrational than some of the more hidebound theories of thrift or of getting rich by saving.

No one can become rich merely by saving. Putting aside a sum each week or month in a sock at no interest, or in a savings bank at ordinary interest, will not provide enough for old age unless life in the meantime be rigorously skimped down to the level of mere existence. And if everyone skimped in any such fashion then the country would be so poor that living at all would hardly be worth while.

Unless we have consumption we shall not have production. Production and consumption go together and a rigid national program of saving would, if carried beyond a point, make for general poverty, for there would be no consumption to call new wealth into being.

Therefore, savings must be looked at not as a present deprivation in order to enjoy more in the future, but as a constructive method of increasing not only one's future but also one's present income.

Saving may be a virtue if undertaken as a kind of mental and moral discipline, but such a course of saving is not to be regarded as a financial plan. Constructive saving in order to increase one's income is a financial operation and to be governed by financial rules; disciplinary saving is another matter entirely. The two have been confused.

Most of the old precepts contrasting the immorality of speculation with the morality of sound investment have no basis in fact. They just have so often been repeated as true that they are taken as true. If one buys a debt—that is, takes a secure bond or mortgage at a fixed rate of interest—then that is supposed to be an investment. In the case of the debt, the principal sum as well as the interest is fixed and the investor cannot get more than he contracts for. The law guards against getting more and also it regulates the procedure by which the lender can take the property of the borrower in case of default. But the law cannot say that the property of the debtor will be worth the principal sum of the debt when it falls due; the creditor must take that chance.

The investor in a debt strictly limits his possible gain, but he does not limit his loss. He speculates against the interest rate. If his security pays 4 per cent and money is worth 6 or 7 percent then he is lending at less than the current rate; if money is worth 3 per cent then he is lending at more than he could otherwise get.

The buyer of a common share in an enterprise limits neither his gains nor his losses. However, he excludes one element of speculation—the change in the value of money. For whatever earnings he gets will be in current money values. If he buys shares in a wholly new and untried enterprise, then his hazards are great, but if he buys into established enterprises, then he takes no more chance than does the investor who buys a debt.

It is difficult to see why a bond or mortgage should be considered as a more conservative investment than a good stock, for the only difference in practice is that the bond can never be worth more than its face value or return more than the interest, while a stock can be worth more than was paid for it and can return a limitless profit.

One may lose on either a bond or a stock. If a company fails it will usually be reorganized and in that case the bonds will have to give way to new money and possibly they will be scaled down. The common stock holders may lose all, or again they may get another kind of stock which may or may not eventually have a value. In a failure, neither the bond-holders nor the stockholders will find any great cause for happiness—but there are very few failures among the large corporations.

Beneficial Borrowing

A first mortgage on improved real estate is supposedly a very safe in-vestment, but the value of realty shifts quickly and even the most expe-rienced investors in real-estate mortgages have to foreclose an appreciable percentage of their mortgages and buy in the properties to protect themselves. It may be years before the property can be sold again.

I would rather buy real estate than buy mortgages on it, for then I have the chance of gaining more than I paid. On a mortgage I cannot get back more than I lend, but I may get back less.

The line between investment and speculation is a very hazy one, and a definition is not to be found in the legal form of a security or in limiting the possible return on the money. The difference is rather in the ap proach.

Placing a bet is very different from placing one's money with a cor-poration which has thoroughly demonstrated that it can normally earn profits and has a reasonable expectation of earning greater profits. This may be called speculation, but it would be more accurate to think of the operation as going into business with men who have demonstrated that they know how to do business.

The old view of debt was quite as illogical as the old view of invest-ment. It was beyond the conception of anyone that debt could be con-structive. Every old saw about debt and there must be a thousand of them—is bound up with borrowing instead of earning. We now know that borrowing may be a method of earning and beneficial to everyone concerned. Suppose a man needs a certain amount of money in order to buy a set of tools or anything else which will increase his income. He can take one of two courses. He can save the money and in the course of time buy his tools, or he can, if proper facilities are provided, borrow the money at a reasonable rate of interest, buy the tools and immediately so increase his income that he can pay off his debt and own the tools within half the time that it would have taken him to save the money and pay cash. The loan enables him at once to create more wealth than before and consequently makes him a more valuable citizen. By increasing his power to produce he also increases his power to consume and therefore he increases the power of others to produce in order to fill his new needs and naturally to increase their power to consume, and so on and on. By borrowing the money instead of saving it he increases the ability to save and steps up prosperity at once.

The Way to Wealth

That is exactly what the automobile has done to the prosperity of the country through the plan of installment payments. The installment plan of paying for automobiles, when it was first launched, ran counter to the old notions of debt. It was opposed by bankers, who saw in it only an incentive for extravagance. It was opposed by manufacturers because they thought people would be led to buy automobiles instead of their products.

The results have been exactly opposite to the prediction. The ability to buy automobiles on credit gave an immediate step-up to their purchase. Manufacturing them, serving them, building roads for them to run on, and caring for the people who used the roads have brought into existence about ten billion dollars of new wealth each year—which is roughly about the value of the farm crops. The creation of this new wealth gave a large increase to consumption and has brought on our present very solid prosperity.

But without the facility for going into debt or the facility for the consumer's getting credit—call it what you will—this great addition to wealth might never have taken place and certainly not for many years to come. Debt may be a burden, but it is more likely to be an incentive.

The great wealth of this country has been gained by the forces of production and consumption pushing each other for supremacy. The personal fortunes of the country have been made not by saving but by producing.

Mere saving is closely akin to the socialist policy of dividing and likewise runs up against the same objection that there is not enough around to save. The savings that count cannot be static. They must be going into the production of wealth. They may go in as debt and the managers of the wealth-making enterprises take all of the profit over and above the interest paid. That has been the course recommended for saving and for the reasons that have been set out—the fallacy of conservative investment which is not conservative at all.

The way to wealth is to get into the profit end of wealth production in this country.

THE CRASH OF THE STOCK MARKET

The following article is similar to many that appeared in the last days of October 1929. After the first collapse of the market on October 24, a group of bankers organized by financier J. P. Morgan created a pool of money to shore up stock prices. Their heavy buying worked partially for the moment, and they began quietly unloading the stocks they had bought. But an even worse crash came on October 29.

The article expresses a mixture of fear and optimism. There seemed little choice but to make statements and gestures of confidence. To do anything else would only have made the panic worse. Even most of those who did not honestly expect a recovery did not expect serious long-term financial trouble for the nation. It was true that many companies and individuals had been ruined, but, after all, market prices as a whole had merely dropped to about the 1927 level. To many people market collapses were painful but essentially healthy adjustments of the economy. Unsound companies went broke, and overpriced stocks returned to reasonable levels. Other crashes had had only temporary effects. Gradually, however, people realized that recovery was not happening. Instead business failures continued and unemployment became much worse. The country was sliding into the worst depression in its history.

FROM "STOCKS COLLAPSE IN 16,410,030-SHARE DAY, BUT
RALLY AT CLOSE CHEERS BROKERS; BANKERS OPTIMISTIC, TO
CONTINUE AID"
(*New York Times*, October 30, 1929)

• • •

Efforts to estimate yesterday's market losses in dollars are futile because of the vast number of securities quoted over the counter and on out-of-town exchanges on which no calculations are possible. However, it was estimated that 880 issues, on the New York Stock Exchange, lost between $8,000,000,000 and $9,000,000,000 yesterday. Added to that is to be reckoned the depreciation on issues on the Curb Market, in the over the counter market and on other exchanges.

Two Extra Dividends Declared

There were two cheerful notes, however, which sounded through the pall of gloom which overhung the financial centres of this country. One was the brisk rally of stocks at the close, on tremendous buying by those who believe that prices have sunk too low. The other was that the liquidation has been so violent, as well as widespread, that many bankers, brokers and industrial leaders expressed the belief last night that it now had run its course.

A further note of optimism in the soundness of fundamentals was sounded by the directors of the United States Steel Corporation and the American Can Company, each of which declared an extra dividend of $1 a share at their late afternoon meetings.

Banking support, which would have been impressive and successful under ordinary circumstances, was swept violently aside, as block after block of stock, tremendous in proportions, deluged the market. Bid prices placed by bankers, industrial leaders and brokers trying to halt the decline were crashed through violently, their orders were filled, and quotations plunged downward in a day of disorganization, confusion and financial impotence.

Change Is Expected Today

That there will be a change today seemed likely from the statements made last night by financial and business leaders. Organized support will be accorded to the market from the start, it is believed, but those who are staking their all on the country's leading securities are placing a great deal of confidence, too, in the expectation that there will be an overnight change in sentiment; that the counsel of cool heads will prevail and that the mob psychology which has been so largely responsible for the market's debacle will be broken.

STUDY QUESTIONS

1. How often does the green light appear in *The Great Gatsby*? Does it stand for anything more than money? If so, what?

2. Some of Raskob's advice about stock investment is more or less what you would get today from popular writers about the market—from Peter Lynch, for example. Some of Raskob's advice seems convincing, but does any of it seem too good to be true? If so, what?

3. Imagine the reaction of someone like George Wilson to Raskob's advice. What do you think it would be?

4. Imagine Tom Buchanan's reaction to Raskob's article. What would it be?

5. When you see the title "Everybody Ought to Be Rich," does it appeal to you, or does it put you on your guard? Explain.

6. Do you think that today's reactions to an article titled "Everybody Ought to Be Rich" would be different from what they were in 1929? If so, different in what ways?

7. Does any of Raskob's advice sound convincing to you? If so, what?

8. Raskob and a few men like him were largely responsible for the increase in automobile ownership in the 1920s. Very few things have changed American life as much as has the automobile. In *The Great Gatsby* the automobile is very important, both practically and symbolically. How is it important in the relations between Jordan Baker and Nick Carraway? Pay special attention to what they say to each other.

9. In what ways are cars essential to the plot of the novel?

10. What does Nick say about Tom and Daisy and their money near the end of the novel? What significance do you think Fitzgerald wants you to find in his comment?

11. Gatsby says that Daisy's voice is "full of money." Notice carefully how her voice sounds to Nick Carraway. What significance do you think Nick finds in her voice?

12. Are Nick and Gatsby saying the same things about Daisy's voice in different ways? Explain.

13. When Myrtle Wilson criticizes her husband at the party, for what does she criticize him? What does this say about her values?

14. Fitzgerald once thought of calling his novel "Among Ash Heaps and Millionaires." Do you think this says more about the book than the title *The Great Gatsby*? Explain.

15. Do you see any significance in the fact that Nick Carraway is learning the bond business? Where else do bonds appear in the novel?

TOPICS FOR WRITTEN OR ORAL EXPLORATION

1. Imagine that it is October 30, 1929, and that you have just read the *New York Times* article. A substantial amount of your money is invested in stocks. You do not know the future. All you have is the article. You are discussing the situation with your family. What are you going to say and do?

2. A good part of Daisy's appeal for Gatsby is her money, and yet he does not want her for her money. He will not approach her until he has money of his own. What do you think money—especially Daisy's money—means to Gatsby?

3. Discuss what you think money means to other characters—to Nick Carraway and Tom Buchanan, for example.

4. The people at the economic level of those at Myrtle Wilson's party are likely to have bought into the trusts Raskob wished to create. Imagine a party in 1931 where they discuss the situation.

5. It is unlikely that someone like Tom Buchanan would be wiped out by the Depression, although he might have been hurt badly. How would he have reacted to the Depression?

6. Create your own scenario. The Wilsons are still alive at the end of the novel. What happened to them during the Depression?

SUGGESTIONS FOR FURTHER READING

A very good chapter on the 1929 stock market crash appears in Frederick Lewis Allen's *Only Yesterday: An Informal History of the 1920's* (New York: Harper and Row, 1931).

Geoffrey Perrett's *America in the Twenties: A History* (New York: Simon and Schuster, 1987) is an excellent source for background on this period.

Page Smith's *Redeeming the Time: A People's History of the 1920's and the New Deal* (New York: McGraw-Hill, 1987) is also an excellent background book.

6 _____

The Great Gatsby
Then and Now

The Great Gatsby is, in one sense, a period piece. It captures the mood, the feeling, of a time in United States history. Yet it is much more than that. It survives as a compelling story in spite of the fact that conditions of American life have changed drastically since it was written. Like all great books, it rises above its historical context. Although knowledge of the background adds dimension to the novel, it can stand very well without it.

The garish, frenetic world of the 1920s is gone. Organized crime, for example, is unfortunately still with us, but to one of Gatsby's contemporaries it would now be unrecognizable. We rarely see screaming headlines telling us how gangsters have shot each other. The mobs are quieter and better organized than they once were. The goose that laid the golden eggs, Prohibition, has long since disappeared, but gangs unobtrusively deal in gambling, prostitution, drugs, and some legitimate businesses. Their leaders no longer capture the popular imagination as did Arnold Rothstein, Al Capone, and Dutch Schultz.

It is revealing that gangster films today are more likely to be set in the 1920s than later. There has never been a flood of gangster films to match that of the late 1920s and very early 1930s. The modern gangster is a relatively dull fellow.

The reaction to sports, too, lacks the wild imagination and almost hysterical hero worship of the 1920s. Rarely is the sort of attention Gertrude Ederle received lavished on a modern athlete. It is hard to imagine a modern boy standing before an athlete guilty of taking a bribe, pleading "Say it ain't so, Joe." Modern athletes perhaps lead lives as colorful as those of earlier ones, but they lack the colorful public images of Babe Ruth or Jack Dempsey.

The same naive idealism that drove Gatsby made Americans yearn for heroes and search for them everywhere—in crime, in sports, in politics, and in business. Young Americans wanted to reach the very pinnacle of conventional success—or at least were made to feel that they should want to. The epigraph to Fitzgerald's play, *The Vegetable*, a quotation from H. L. Mencken, parodies this idea: "Any man who doesn't want to get on in the world, to make a million dollars, and maybe even park his tooth brush in the White House, hasn't got as much to him as a good dog has—he's nothing more or less than a vegetable."

Young Americans today are still ambitious, but this particular kind of ambition is now a rare exception rather than a general rule. Professors who have read hundreds or even thousands of introductory themes know that freshmen want careers and money, and that they look forward to new friends and new experiences. But very few aim for the presidency or a mansion like Gatsby's.

In politics, too, public attitudes have changed—perhaps much more than the realities of politics have changed. Nan Britton claimed in *The President's Daughter* (1930) that Harding was the father of her illegitimate child; she believed that she conceived the child in the cloakroom of the United States Senate. Among those tainted with corruption was the secretary of the interior, who was convicted of taking bribes.

Since Harding's administration, corruption in high places has continued. The public has since been exposed to countless salacious stories about later presidents. President Kennedy supposedly kept up an active extramarital love life while he was in the White House. It is common knowledge that Franklin Roosevelt had an extramarital affair. President Clinton was faced with charges of sexual harassment brought by Paula Corbin Jones. Even staid President Eisenhower reportedly thought seriously about leaving his wife for a woman he fell in love with while commanding Allied forces during World War II.

As for financial and political corruption, President Clinton has had to fight off potentially incriminating charges growing out of the Whitewater investigation. Vice President Gore's fundraising activities have been investigated by a committee of the United States Senate. Both Republicans and Democrats are under fire because of the size and nature of the political contributions they accept. Nothing in Harding's administration compares to the Watergate scandal, in which Richard Nixon, a sitting president of the United States, stepped down to avoid being tried before the United States Senate on charges of obstructing justice. Major officials of his administration were sent to prison.

Is the world of politics and finance, then, more or less what it was when Gatsby said he was "able to do the [police] commissioner a favor once" (73)? There is one vitally important difference. The public of Gatsby's time was not yet shockproof. Only a scandal the size of Watergate can now hold public attention as Teapot Dome once held it. Stories about Whitewater or about possibly illegal campaign contributions produce nothing but yawns from the general public. The naiveté and easily outraged idealism of the 1920s are gone. *The Great Gatsby* is about American innocence, not just Gatsby's. The innocence has long since departed.

Gatsby's ultimate innocence lies in his love for Daisy Buchanan, or, rather, in the form that love takes. Gatsby's love is almost a caricature of what were then common attitudes. Middle class and upper class women were expected to be objects of worship. Economically marginal themselves, they inspired men to achieve and produce. Their role was to spend money conspicuously but with taste. These women were in the very dangerous and stressful position of being idealized and yet being dependent on the men who idealized them. It is hardly surprising that men often felt betrayed when women did not live up to the ideal, or that women who resented their position found ways to take their revenge.

Fitzgerald's heroines, from first to last, are economically vulnerable, unless, like Nicole Warren of *Tender Is the Night*, they are independently wealthy. Rosemary Hoyt, a major figure but not the heroine in *Tender Is the Night*, is a successful film actress who is once described as being a "boy" economically. Most of Fitzgerald's heroines are dangerous or at least tragically disappointing to the men who love them.

The heroine of Fitzgerald's final novel, *The Love of the Last Tycoon*, is modeled on the highly ambitious, career-oriented Sheilah

Graham, but these qualities do not come through in Fitzgerald's creation. Graham had been brought up in poverty in England and was already a very competitive Hollywood columnist when she and Fitzgerald became lovers. There is no sign that her fictional counterpart, Kathleen Moore, has any professional ambitions. *The Love of the Last Tycoon* was unfinished at the time of Fitzgerald's death, so in spite of his notes and outlines, one can only guess what final form he would have given it.

Almost certainly, though, the ending would have included the death of the hero, Monroe Stahr, a brilliant Hollywood producer in love with Kathleen Moore. Stahr first sees her during an accidental flooding of a studio when she is sitting on a floating statue of Siva, the Indian god of both love and death. This heavy-handed symbolism leads the reader to expect that she will be as destructive as some of Fitzgerald's earlier heroines.

Modern readers of Fitzgerald sometimes have difficulty understanding his heroines, or tend to assume that their behavior is a reflection of his life with Zelda. (In part it is, but it is much more than that.) In very fundamental ways our society has changed. Few people would claim that American women now have complete equality with men. As of this writing the median salary for women is just under 75 percent of what it is for men. Scattered headlines about the "glass ceiling" show that women still have difficulty in reaching the top positions in most professions. Yet there is one crucial difference between women's position in the 1990s and their position in the 1920s. Just as there once was an unspoken assumption that women with meaningful jobs or careers were freaks, now it is taken for granted that women will have these things.

Current popular fiction and entertainment are filled with women characters doing work that once was done only by men. The old notion that a woman's only career and livelihood came to her through her husband is now gone. Most of the male-female relations in Fitzgerald's work are based on a kind of female dependency that has been greatly modified, if it has not ceased to exist.

It would seem, then, that Fitzgerald speaks to the reader from a world so different as to be incomprehensible. Yet nearly all readers of *The Great Gatsby* would agree that he does not. The reason is that Gatsby's failed and misguided idealism reaches far beyond the limitations of American culture in the 1920s. If contemporary readers lack the naive idealism and accompanying disillusionment of Gatsby's world, they still empathize with his plight, just as Western culture, at least since the Renaissance, has empathized with the madness of Don Quixote, for Gatsby is a direct descendant of Don Quixote. The dreamer, the disappointed lover—this is someone nearly everybody understands. The Roaring Twenties is the ideal setting for Gatsby's story, but it is only the setting. The story itself is as vital as ever.

Index

About the Authors

DALTON GROSS is Professor of English at Southwest Texas State University. He has a special interest in the literary and social milieu of the United States in the 1920s. With MaryJean Gross, he has contributed twelve biographies to *American National Biography* (forthcoming) and seven to the *Encyclopedia of American Literature* (forthcoming), and has written articles on *The Great Gatsby* for *Notes and Queries* and *The Explicator*.

MARYJEAN GROSS is Assistant Professor of English at Southwest Texas State University. She has a special interest in the history of the novel, with emphasis on nineteenth-century British fiction. With Dalton Gross, she has contributed twelve biographies to *American National Biography* (forthcoming) and seven to the *Encyclopedia of American Literature* (forthcoming), and has written articles on *The Great Gatsby* for *Notes and Queries* and *The Explicator*.